I0437452

REBIRTHING THE AMERICAN DREAM

CELEBRATING INAUGURATION OF BARACK HUSSEIN OBAMA, 44TH PRESIDENT OF THE UNITED STATES OF AMERICA

Dudley Bennett

authorHOUSE®

AuthorHouse™
1663 Liberty Drive
Bloomington, IN 47403
www.authorhouse.com
Phone: 1-800-839-8640

© *2009 Dudley Bennett. All rights reserved.*

No part of this book may be reproduced, stored in a retrieval system, or transmitted by any means without the written permission of the author.

First published by AuthorHouse 6/8/2009

ISBN: 978-1-4389-8997-6 (e)
ISBN: 978-1-4389-8841-2 (sc)
ISBN: 978-1-4389-8842-9 (hc)

Library of Congress Control Number: 2009905179

Printed in the United States of America
Bloomington, Indiana

This book is printed on acid-free paper.

CHAPTER REVIEW

Chapter One

Rebirthing the American Dream 1

Our beloved country is at a crossroads. Economic and cultural failure raises the question who are we as a country and what is our destiny. We are people committed to the pursuit of justice, caring for all people, and expanding education. We pursue the American Dream for ourselves and as a model for the whole world.

Chapter Two

Soul Is Destiny 13

Love is the ubiquitous life force seeking expression within all beings. Soul is the source of human greatness. It participates in the energy field surrounding and informing all sentient life. Soul is the most trustworthy part of us. The Experience of soul is the ultimate assurance of life's blessings.

Chapter Three

Integrity Is Being Whole And Complete 21

The world is not two of anything. In this non-dualistic world scientists and saints promote physical and metaphysical agendas that are strangely similar. From a monist point of view the world's laws, values, and norms are integrated into a single whole. Personal integrity is a matter of discovering and expressing that singularity.

Chapter Four

Life Force Is Love 37

The universe is created as living theater of consciousness manifesting the life force. We are immersed in the drama of life. The practice of prayer, intention, and volition bring forth emerging meaning and blessings. Love is the in-channeling and out-flowing of the life force in human affairs. By its power it enlightens the mind, inflames the soul, inspires arts, and contains the visions of the destiny of the race.

INTRODUCTION

You cannot overcome a free people. When threat is real and goals are clear, each citizen in his position and station in life will undertake responsible action in behalf of the homeland. Marching to the same drummer they will overcome obstacles and achieve the right. We have done it before and will do it again. Sitting quietly in the study, meditating, reflecting, and writing this collection of essays is one patriots contribution to our common purpose.

Culture is the way of life of a group of people that includes behaviors, beliefs, values, symbols, and rituals. The core of culture is formed by values members accept without thinking about them. Events, institutions, and individuals are judged on scales of good-evil and right-wrong. Most people are passive to these matters and become what they learn. Values form the collective unconscious that distinguishes one group of people from another. By communication and imitation group values and norms are passed along generation to generation. In a democracy through discussion and debate cultural values are subject to observation study and modification.

Depending on the viability of its values a culture maintains itself or suffers entropy. Recently our beloved country has shown debilitation. The current financial crisis makes clear the idea of the mystique of the market place and the unfettered wizardry of a few executives who became immensely rich at the expense of the many is not acceptable. With clear statement of probity and financial policy, to meet entrepreneurial needs of the nation and calm wheeling and dealing, greater oversight will be necessary.

The value and actions of our beloved country suggest a dystopian trend.

> Banality of commercial culture and free market fantasy
> Ubiquitous exploitation of sex for profit
> Ability to overlook repression and pain of world children
> Deploying military throughout the globe with unclear purpose
> Political power of the military-industrial complex
> Ruinous level of national debt
> Deterioration of the value of our currency
> Media culture broadcast into living rooms replace vital institutions
> Decay of traditional institutions.

The election of President Obama in 2008 has made clear our country has entered a transitional state of large change to our institutions. We have had first hand knowledge of the consequences of values like greed, anger, pride, injustice, and absence of mercy. Small wonder they are called deadly. Under the new administration we seek to propound values written in the conscience of humans as they relate to education, rule of law, frugality, simplicity, compassion, and justice. We cherish this opportunity to recreate the expectation of greatness that empowered our forefathers.

In this effort I find myself in a rising tide of media articles by those unwilling to accept rationalizations for terrorism, slavery, and war. Friends and associates have joined the effort to enlarge the soul of mankind. In particular I wish to acknowledge Marcia Bennett for her untiring support in our search for meaning. My beloved children Paul, Martha, and Sarah plus grandchildren Michael, Rehanna, Daniel, Aly, and Kira often, despite themselves, are a major source of inspiration and verve. Mary and Steve Burkhammer continually teach me about healing at a distance. Jean Brown is mentor to many of us who no longer cite a creed. Friend Bernie Shagan MD assembles a Minion of Metaphysicians who meet regularly to ferret out the depths of reality.

For the reader I trust these essays will open the door for a glimpse of a larger vision.

CHAPTER ONE

REBIRTHING THE AMERICAN DREAM

The inauguration of Barack Hussein Obama as 44th President of the United States brings new hope to a morally and economically tattered nation. Citizens are palpably excited about the election that elevated this calm and clear headed citizen to the highest office of the land. Equally moving, was the recent celebration of the 40th anniversary of the death of Martin Luther King Jr. of blessed memory. His "I have a dream" vision of a free people burst out of his heart on the steps of the Lincoln Monument and continues to inspire generations.[1] As citizens of a democracy we know we are responsible for our beloved country both its conception and fulfillment. We walk in the footsteps of great men.

> We hold these truths to be self-evident; that all men are created equal; that they are endowed by their creator with certain unalienable rights; that among these are life, liberty, and the pursuit of happiness...[2]

With this vision embedded in our hearts, whatever position and station we hold in life, with hard work, innovation, and quick learning, we will fashion new approaches to vexing challenges. We do this to prove ourselves worthy of our great heritage. My intention, to the

---

[1] August 28, 1963
[2] Declaration Of Independence July 4,1776

best of my abilities, is to fulfill my duties as citizen. This collection of essays is designed to put citizens in touch with their deeper selves, unlock their greatness, allow them to regain control of their destiny in order to benefit mankind. When marching in the same direction, a free people are undefeatable.

I intend for my countrymen to experience depth of soul and paths of honor. We shall create classes, schools and institutions to bring this about. What I desire you see lies beyond ordinary sense perception. I delve here into the spiritual nature of life and immortality. In approaching the indescribable reader must wonder and wander a bit in places not usually visited by ordinary consciousness. I am impelled by a larger vision to discover and rebirth the dream that made America great.

I join those who argue for the sanctity of human life. Surrounded by ugliness and violence we have much to rise above in order to promote human dignity and equality. Life is not a game in which competition eclipses cooperation and we are known by our absurdities. Rather our short stay under the sun is an opportunity to recreate the expectation of greatness that empowered our forefathers. Holy writ counsels: "Honor all men, love the brotherhood, reverence God… "[3]

Three fundamental ways of viewing the world include Mechanistic Materialism, Mythic Ritualism, and Metaphysical Monism. While they evolved historically, all three can be seen in any age, and most vividly in our own.

---

[3]   I Peter 2:17

MECHANISTIC MATERIALISM	RITUALISTIC MYSTICISM	METAPHYSICAL MONISM
Machinery	Mortal Mind	Life Force
Cause and Effect	Abstract Concepts	100 % Energy
Inductive	Deductive	Illusion of Physical
Values Instinctive	Solipsism	Wave/Particle Duality
Meaning Absent	Future Oriented	Infinite Possibilities
Jungle Metaphor Survival Mod	Rationalizations Prominent	Time Reversal Symmetry
	Heroes, Gods, Sacred Events	Conscious Creation of Future
A Posteriori	A Priori	

Mechanistic Materialism

Once sent in motion and governed by the immutable laws of cause and effect the world proceeds to a random and chaotic end. German pessimist philosopher Arthur Schopenhauer (1788-1860) said at its core the universe is not a rational place.[4] In a world of endless strife that has no meaning the best path is to minimize desire, value the quiescent aesthetic, and moral life. When life is a jungle and values instinctive, survival is the only concern. Newtonian mechanistic materialism asserting a closed universe indifferent to human effort inadequately explains the continuous vigor of the world.

---

[4]   Arthur Schopenhauer <u>The World As Will And Representation</u> 1818

Ritualistic Mysticism

Stories about supernatural beings, sacred ancestors and heroes employed to explain the nature of the world, human psychology, and social customs are no longer compelling. Whatever its pretentions for truth and revealed wisdom too often religion has become another snout at the public trough of political and financial advancement. Placing rationalization above reason, physical above metaphysical, survival above honor, the institution makes itself adjunct to the powerful. When indifferent to the pain of others it appears able and ready to promote injustice, conflict, and terrorism.

There is irony in no-compromise theology. Human destiny, it avows, depends solely on divine providence who before time began predestined individuals to heaven or hell. Revealed in holy writ, religious doctrines are not open to investigation, discussion, and testing. It is alleged that due to its own corruption mankind suffers original sin. It is argued man is placed on earth for the sole purpose of glorifying God not obsessing on earthly problems. While humans deserve eternal damnation, an inscrutable God grants Grace of salvation to an elect few.

Making God arbitrary and vindictive is blasphemy. To dismiss the life force as empty drama is too facile. To reduce human discourse to ritual display is too banal. To overlook the elegance and depth of the cosmos is too shallow. To obviate tension between good and evil is too simple. Life is real. It is not practice. In pain and joy we participate with that which is coming into being. Not arbitrary adjuncts, the human soul is at the heart of the business of creation. What we do here is to discover our true destiny.

Metaphysical Monism

Reality is a unified whole and all things are part of a single existent consciousness. Monism is a nexus between ancient Gnosticism and contemporary physics. A paradigm is emerging, enabling us to deepen our understanding of the universe and the role of human consciousness. We are on the verge of a new incarnation on the planet where individuals share in the creative power of the life force and bring about the much dreamed of peaceable kingdom.

Physicists tell us the world is composed of waves of possibilities and probabilities that do not exist in space and time and have no objective content. It is indeed mysterious that waves collapse and become elemental particles of the physical when observed by man or machine. When there is an observer in the equation the physical world comes into being. In the wave/ particle duality, we cannot know what is going on in the waves because only what we see is visible to us. While the collapse has a machine like nature, it takes a conscious person to set up the apparatus, observe and measure the results.

All matter is connected to the farthest reaches of the universe. All sentient life shares consciousness and participates in the field of boundless possibilities. Moment to moment, the aware person shares the dimensionless underpinnings of the micro and macro universes. There is vast physical and metaphysical power in calm abiding. Through the process of intention the human spirit is a powerful tool to influence reality. Artists, saints, and musicians who spent their days and lives in prayer, work, and retrospection have produced much good for mankind.

The reality we face daily is not what it appears to be. Consciousness is the unseen power in the world in which we live. When consciousness enters matter it creates mind which is the secret underground of existence and the realm from which we come. As a fundamental part of the universe, we were born to be involved in reality and influence it. In some supernatural way we put our understanding into the world.

Countrymen must awaken to challenges at the beginning of the Second Millennium. Life on the planet has a phantasmagorical quality as fanatics seek to destroy unbelievers by waging terrorist wars. The peace-loving majority, distracted by sports and pleasure, cannot sit back and let it happen. The peaceful majority in Russia let the Communists murder about 20 million people. Chinese Communists killed a staggering 70 million people. German genocide destroyed 6 million Jews. During World War II Japanese slaughtered their way across South East Asia killing 12 million by sword, shovel, and bayonet. Rwanda collapses in butchery.

Holding life to be a jungle where only the fittest survive, the neighbor becomes predator. When survival and comfort are paramount, fascist leadership expand its geopolitical domain by enslaving others. Irrational fierceness drives the zealot, fanatic, and terrorist. Secrecy, deceit, double-talk and violence are means to social control. To amass power it makes sense to conflate the sacred and holy with the barbarous. Reason put in service of warfare, becomes a casualty itself.

Let us awaken from our stupor and no longer tolerate fanatics who seek to rule the world through fear, boasting of their desire for a martyrs death, and welcoming the end of the world. As free people let us resist fanatics who bomb, behead, murder, and butcher the innocent. We must obviate those who teach their young to kill and become suicide bombers. Not misled by pious slogans, we shall not surrender honor nor be cowed by threat. Let us not sit aside indifferent to life and death matters.

We are in danger today of forfeiting the precious legacy of liberty bequeathed by our founding fathers. With an inspired view of the ordinary man's ability to rule themselves, our founders created a self-correcting system of checks and balances that has protected us from tyranny for 200 years. Today this system is in crisis not from inquisitions, feudal monarchs, or mischievous nobles, but from the cynical view that national problems are too complex and change too rapid, that it is beyond an ordinary citizens capacity to understand much less to act through channels of republican government.

Leaders arrogate increasing authority to act on personal and individual motivations unconcerned with the outcome for the rest of us. While assuring they have our best interests in mind, they subvert civil liberties and close down open society. Human self-determination is a thrilling and radical idea; transforming human society vastly increases human potential.

Citizens are not commodities. They are not just consumers. Let us elevate our sights and mount a higher vision of citizenship than the mercantile idea of endless consumption. Driven by the current fad or fashion they are encouraged to buy and spend, leading to indebtedness. It becomes unpatriotic not to consume since economics is the central way we relate to the rest of the world. Social status and rank are determined by the size of a persons bank account, stock portfolio, and mansion.

Let us commit ourselves to creating a country that models the rule of law, promotes education and science, and furthers world-wide peace. America is bright city on a hill, a beacon that models justice and compassion for the rest of the world.

> Lets us cherish sacred honor,
> Abide peacefully in life and death.
> Calm self with silence of the field.
> Do no harm.
> See yourself essential part of the whole.
> In conflict not loose sight of your destiny,
> Spiritualize, all of it, always
> Reverence and value life in all its forms.
> Take responsibility for all of it.
> Source energetic healing for others,
> Rejoice in the arts,
> Practice tenderness and compassion.

By indifference we participate in degrading the human enterprise and passively support evil. Founding fathers held out the dream for citizens to be responsible for themselves, each other, and the nation. As citizens we must work to keep alive the splendid and unprecedented experiment in human self-determination. Be alert to these anti-democratic moves such as are included in the diagram below.

Soldiers deployed in residential areas
Rule of law replaced with rendition, incarceration and torture
War as a tool of geo-politics
Judge, lawyers, and lawmakers barred from office
Muzzling of the free press
Blacked out media networks

Restriction of travel
Critics threatened
Identify cards used for surveillance

When you see these know it is time for a new civil rights movement. We must resist forces that distance citizens from protections of the Constitution. Use every opportunity to define and resist fascist tendencies aimed at glorifying the state and increasing control of citizen ambitions.

When we become fully conscious we recognize our spiritual heritage and see the common potential in all mankind to heal and transform. Mutual recognition is the realization that all beings share the same life force. All are able to manifest love, build trust, proclaim forgiveness, and serve the common good. We dare not recognize the divine imprimatur in each other, or be dissuaded by fear. God confronted Cain by asking" Where is your brother?" Cain replies with the off-putting line of the self-absorbed who turn their backs on the poor and oppressed in the world saying "Am I my brother's keeper?"[5] Living secure with material abundance the indifferent allow themselves to believe others are distant others and not real beings like themselves. Turning away from strangers, denying their right to be cared for, is to disaffirm and disallow the life force in ourselves and others. To tolerate persecution and destruction of others is to deny our own personal integrity and honor.

The life force embedded in us is the inherent movement toward goodness and holiness. It is a force for transformation and healing fitting our present state of evolution. Our task is to bring forth aspects of ourselves that have always been there. Recognizing the universality of the life force is the defining moment in an individual's life. Nothing is fundamentally missing from the human experience. Reality is not piecemeal; it is all here and perfect just the way it is. By elevating our sights and recognizing our self-constituted ability to reflect love and healing, we become part of the creative and redemptive energy both inside and outside of us.

---

[5]   Genesis 4:9

American Dream

Let us rebuild the American dream of small self-contained functioning communities spread across the nation composed of ethnic family structures. A place where individual moral and social ethical values are vibrant and alive within individuals and their institutions. Where the value of something can be ascertained. Where institutions are scaled to the human size. Where the false idol of wealth has no devotees. Where education built on the humanities, arts, and science fosters transcendent visions for humanity. Where healers garner citizen love and respect. Where life and death are cherished in the daily activities of citizens.

When able to quiet retro and neo minds and are without bodily disturbance, individuals align with the ganzfeld and experience peace, equanimity, and joy. They have a sense of omniscience and participation at the heart of the life force. External oriented life driven by desire to wealth, power, and position recedes and is replaced by a conscious desire to be a source of healing during a finite visit to this planet. High lighting the life force gives meaning to mortality. Rather than manifesting absurdity, our "three score and ten" are our part of possibility which sentient life is.

The scale and complexity of problems today call into question the ability of democratic government to frame issues in such a way they lend themselves to meaningful plebiscite. We face strong fascist tendencies from elected officials who experience citizens distance from and impertinence to complex multi-national issues of statecraft. Due to rapidity of change, immediacy of conflict, and rationalizations galore, leaders assurances they act in the best interest of the citizenry are met with dubiety. If we scale down the size of representative government, the hearts and souls of the electorate become pertinent to political discussion and ballot

This America exists. Let us hold up the rural community as model of what we seek for future generations. Democratic communities join in representative State government. State Officials meeting in the national capital create a federal configuration to further, not world-wide hegemony, but functional values of included communities. This life respecting model where the power of love replaces the lust for power will inevitably attract others.

The future we seek involves rethinking who we are as citizens. How can we maintain democratic values in representative government? Our 200 year history has taught us much about what to avoid and what may lie in our best interests. We do not worship at the altar of the false god of world-wide sovereignty. With proper education and support we assume all cultures, nations and ethnic groups can find their own place in the sun.

In becomes increasingly clear, with or without slave labor large agglomerations of people are inherently unsustainable. Dystrophic tendencies are everywhere visible. In the not too distant future large cities will stand abandoned as monuments to a failed culture reminiscent of Babylonian Ziggurats, Mayan Temples, Egyptian Pyramids, and Castles lurking along the Rhine. As entropy increases we shall have to live with increased sense of randomness that will prove hard to digest. We shall have to develop our anthropological studies to develop, a deep inner resource that can lead us out of chaos into a new world of justice and peace.

We will not seek world-wide military hegemony posting military bases throughout the world armed with apocalyptic weaponry hoping fascist fantasy will replace democratic reality. We pass by on the other side of the street from those whose double-talk about the necessity of terrorism and war no longer gain a listening and a thousand rationalizations for harming others are dismissed as banal.

We will not float financial bubbles blown-up by grandees of Wall Street that undermines banking structures maintained by gullible managers and investors for whom wealth is the chief and only meaningful goal in life.

Conscious individuals are emerging everywhere who are unwilling to overlook the genocide and repression of millions upon earth. Beneath the façade of civilization millions succumb to political knavery, disease, hunger, and slavery. This is not acceptable to a free and democratic people. Our goal is to create rural self-maintaining communities where social realities reflect depth of the human spirit in a world aligned with the life force. A place where the measure of success is joy in the smiles of children of all ages.

To reinvigorate the high vision of our American heritage, to complete work of our forefathers, to be responsible for challenges of our own day, let us rethink anthropology and repurpose human intercourse. Like a farmer's field, for it to continue to nourish, liberty demands our sustained attention.

As a contribution to the argument this is a dangerous world. the NYTimes reported [6] two submarines, one French the other British, each carrying 16 nuclear armed missiles collided in the Atlantic on the night of February 3rd, while submerged on patrol. A number of such incidents occurred between western and soviet submarines during the cold war. Another source reported each of these missiles was six times more destructive than the Hiroshima bomb. Public reaction reflected fear the collision could have released vast amounts of radiation across the seabed. No one mentioned the devastation of reason.

Besides the under sea weapons of China, Russia, United States, France and England, there are bunkers of land based weapons. Russia and the United States have something in the order of 10,000 between them. Pakistan, India, are armed and presumably North Korea, and Iran will be shortly.

Extreme secrecy masks the whereabouts on these weapons of mass destruction. The fear of mutual annihilation is thought to be the ultimate defense and reason for maintaining a vast arsenal of weapons of mass destruction. That this makes sense to those in charge staggers the imagination.

Five nations have these apocalyptic devices prowling the depths of the world's sea lanes. Parading the ultimate insanity one commentator said: "these are the strategic crown jewels of the nation…..The are the ultimate tools of national survival in the event of war. Therefore, it

_____

[6]   February 1, 2009

is the very last thing you would share with anybody." Surely this is the ultimate insanity.

Not all known stores of highly enriched uranium are accounted for. Given the cunning of elusive stateless terrorism who can be certain we shall not suffer attacks in metropolitan areas?

CHAPTER TWO

SOUL IS DESTINY

Love is the ubiquitous life force seeking expression within all humans. It is manifested in an individual's search for rectitude and honor and desire to care for others. Love manifests soul and feeling without demand. It uplifts, feels good, and reigns as the harmonizing music of the universe. Through it thinking evolves about the fundamental structure of reality.

Today we are in the midst of revaluating of what is called sacred. In different ages, with disparate models and language, the divine was given contrasting dimensions. It is no longer viable to speak of a moody God who sits in heaven raining down blessing on friends and curses on enemies.

The world is not two of anything. Duality is illusion. There is no division between instrument and music. In a holistic view energy is where in which all aspects of being are revealed. 94% of the universe is composed of energy leaving only 6% matter. Neither adjunct nor afterthought, humans are fields of energy relating to each other and all that is. When energy enters matter it creates consciousness. Humans are fundamentally part of the ambient fields of consciousness. At this level matter recedes and finally disappears. We know and celebrate the life force with every ounce of our being. That liberates powerful insight into death and life.

Things are not what they seem. The obvious is not obvious. That which is easily seen and understood ain't. Quantum Physics demonstrates a single thing can be in two places at the same time and even at great distances instantly influences each other. Remember they are the same thing. If we sit quiet and ponder that, the implications are astounding and far reaching. Everything alive is capable of interacting with and influencing the entirety of an increasingly complex universe. As we move to higher levels of consciousness we think more holistically and perceive life through a perspective in which all things, "live, move, and have their being."[7] As human consciousness expands and matter organizes itself with greater complexity everything is permeated with the life force.

The Psychologist Carl Jung spoke about the soul, as the source of possible human greatness.

> Dream is the small hidden door in the deepest and most hidden sanctum of the soul, which opens into the primal cosmic night that was soul long before there was a conscious ego and will be soul far beyond what conscious ego could ever reach.[8]

When ambient consciousness communicates with us, we receive insight within the limits of our stage in metaphysical growth. Aligned with the life force as much will be revealed to us as we can stand.

The life force within individuals is called soul. Soul is so much a part of us, it convolves mind. To contemplate our relationship to all that is, we sit quietly and reflect at the door of eternity, and we experience an out-of-body moment of truth. We grow in confidence that our formless self is aligned with the essential, beauty, harmony, and intention of creation. As the material world evanesces we have increased confidence in being joined with that which works for good in the cosmos. Holy Writ points to the nature of this insight: "What profiteth a man to gain the whole world and loose his own soul?"[9] The

---

[7]   Acts 17:27
[8]   The meaning of Psychology Vol 10 P 46
[9]   Matthew 16:12

Bhagavad Gita turns this truth another way. "Better ones own duty, though imperfect, than another's duty well performed."[10]

No symbolic description adequately represents that which participates in the ongoing evolution of space/time geometry. In a universe teeming with absurd incongruities of violence and brutality, bringing forth compassion aligns the human endeavor with the intention of the universe and points to the greatness of the human spirit.

Not because they haven't examined the body carefully, or spoke winsomely of it through the ages, locating soul is an evasive business. No one has ever seen soul. Scripture is not helpful in this matter. Paul in the fifth chapter of Thessalonians, verse 23, sees a human trichotomy of body, spirit, and soul. Origen said preexistent soul entered the body as punishment for sin in a previous corporeal state. Following Aristotle, for Thomas Aquinas soul is an individual spiritual substance that takes the form of the body. He taught at death, the soul is severed from the body and leads a separate existence. Creationism argues that original sin in form of the senses is transmitted by parents and human depravity, from which there is no escape, is passed on generation to generation. Not much help here.

Another name for soul is consciousness. Soul is an energy field surrounding and informing all sentient life. When formless soul enters the physical human consciousness is created.

Rather than the rational emotive process being only neurological they are informed by ambient field of consciousness. Mind, memory, and morals rather than being inside people heads, reflect eternal formless energy. The enlightened share consciousness of the cosmos. Accessing the ultra dimension makes unmediated knowledge available The soul is human destiny. This is where metaphysicians dig into reality.

Able to see past everyday events we treasure those artists, musicians, poets, and seers who are able to abstract truth and beauty out of what appears merely banal. Ensouled beings they transform into visual, auditory, and kinesthetic arts the human potential for greatness.

---

[10]   3:35 & 18:47

They see what lies beyond ordinary perception, and feed it back to us in a form that allows glimpses into the high calling of humanity. As we reflect on their work we see auras of that which lies beyond the edges of known reality. In those events in our lives when we experience our deepest selves we have first hand knowledge of our souls. Poets represent the ineffable. Because of its importance in all cultures through all time music is said to be a universal language, speaking things no other form can approach. Consider Edna St. Vincent Millay's

> Sweet sounds, oh, beautiful music do not cease!
> Reject me not into the world again.
> With you alone is excellence and peace,
> Mankind made plausible, his purpose plain,,,,
> This moment is the best the world can give:
> The tranquil blossom on the tortured stem....
> Music my rampart my only one.[11]

With depth of understanding Millay transports us to that transcendent place not accessible by symbolic language. With sacred vision she bespeaks the hidden knowledge of the inner directed.

> The world stands out on either side
> No wider than the heart is wide;
> Above the world is stretched the sky,
> No higher than the soul is high....
> The soul can split the sky in two,
> And let the face of God shine through.[12]

Andrew Wyeth (1917-2009) of the venerated Wyeth art dynasty of Chadds Ford Pennsylvania and Rockland Maine has left a formidable testament to the hidden part of reality. Devotee of realism, his paintings of plain people and ordinary things implied more, indeed much more, than they represented. A vocal patriot his work evoked

---

[11] On Hearing A Symphony of Beethoven
[12] Renaissance

a mythical American agricultural past. "America is absolutely it," he said and lived his entire life.

His raw and evocative Christina's World became an American icon. Disabled from the waist down, she is seen dragging herself across a Maine field "like a crab on a New England shore." To the painter she was a model of a self-sustaining dour and dignified individual living in squalor. He liked the idea unseen figures might be implicit in his work. He once commented Christina's World might be better had he just painted the field and distant house, and the viewer sense Christina's presence without her being there.

Something is unsaid in the picture more powerful than the artists presentation. Hiding behind the picture is the deep, dark, and humorless psyche of Andrew and his haunting equally famous father illustrator NC Wyeth. "I think the great weakness of most of my work, is subject matter. There is too much of it," so says Andrew the mystic.

In his cherished reclusive existence his paintings have a bleak and somber sentiment of unusual depth. He painted snowy fields, diaphanous curtains in open windows, neighbors barns, houses abandoned under leaden skies, fishermen's nets, turkey buzzards, tire tracks. Images that evoked silence, loss, abandonment, absence and desolation.

Something is going on more than meets the eye. He puts things in his work that channels the human spirit. Viewers are attracted by his realism and at the same time sense the emotional abstraction of the artist as clairvoyant. Viewing his oeuvre in the Brandywine River Museum, in a moment of frisson, viewers establish their own relation to what is before them.

In its many expressions and moods, fervent nature reflects something inside human psyche that warms the heart and raises kindly feelings. One cannot improve on Wordsworth.

> My heart leaps us when I behold
>   A rainbow in the sky:
> So was it when my life began,

So it is now I am a man,
So let it be when I shall grow old
Or let me die!
The child is father to the man:
And I could wish my days to be
Bound each to each by natural piety.[13]

Natural piety indeed. In the spirit of fire, lake, stream, forest and sky we know we share the deepest part of all that is. In human desire to love and care for bipeds and quadrupeds the aware person recognizes within himself healing instincts shared with all life forms. Culture based on simplicity and gentleness of this basic soul reality creates education that builds moral fiber and social cohesion. You cannot be enlightened and harm others.

If you look carefully an emanation of goodness can be observed in the lives of individuals with integrity and honor; an aura can be detected surrounding the pure of heart. Pain and confusion are part of life. To those who do not loose heart, the life course reveals the purpose to which they are called. Materialists, dualists, and literalists are wrong. Life is not a predetermined matter indifferent to human effort. Nor is it practice for benefit at some future time and distant place. Life is not practice. This is it. Every day engages us with the issues of beauty, harmony, and healing.

Becoming mindful grows the soul and the individual produces results previously thought to be miraculous. Humankind in micro and macro physics has produced results beyond, indeed way beyond, that previously were thought possible. Precisely because of our scientific prowess we are a threat to ourselves. It is incumbent upon us develop a spiritual underpinning to match threats brought on us by ultra weaponry.

To discuss soul one cannot escape ineffability and paradox. Sensitive individuals receive insight from unknown sources. Soul is the metaphysical space of super-natural perception. The observer influences the ego mind to focus, meditate and reflect on life events.

---

[13]   My Heart Leaps Up

Consciousness is what we experience when the formless enters form. Soul is the channel whereby meaning is shaped to fit a rational apparatus. Walt Whitman invites us all to the effort: "Darest now O soul, walk out with me toward the unknown region, where neither ground is for the feet, nor any path to follow?"[14]

The effort has its own rewards.

> Hark! Hark! My soul angelic songs are swelling
> O'er earth's green fields and oceans wave beat shore
> How sweet the truth these blessed strains are telling
> Of that new life when sin shall be no more.[15]

Soul is the most trustworthy part of us. The experience of soul is assurance of the ultimate blessing life is.

> All you gods who haunt this place give me beauty of inward soul, and may the outward and inward man be one. May I reckon on the wise to be wealthy and may I have such quantity of gold as only the temperate may carry.[16]

---

[14] Darest Now O Soul
[15] Frederick Faber: Pilgrims Of The Night 1854
[16] Plato, Phaedrus 279 BCE

CHAPTER THREE

INTEGRITY IS BEING WHOLE AND COMPLETE

All reality is an expression of one impersonal force that connects and pervades all life forms. Despite appearances of diversity, all manifestations of life are subsumed under the most fundamental character of being. In a non-dualistic world scientists and seers promote physical and metaphysical views that are strangely similar. Under a Monist point of view the world of values, norms and laws are integrated into a single whole. Personal integrity is an expression of that wholeness.

Integrity assumes an individual is whole and complete. An integrated person is internally consistent and empowered by a core set of values aligned with intention of the universe to support life. As an integral part of the universe, in the predicament of life, he can ground himself in the fundamental intention of the universe to produce justice, beauty and meaning.

As citizens we cannot afford to relinquish individual sovereignty and responsibility to socio-political institutions or religious cults. To put aside moral judgment and rational autonomy, to obey leaders bent on their own agendas, abandons the premise of Democracy. To abandon conscience is to succumb to impossibly false dreams.

Integrity refers to the condition of being whole, intact, and complete. The aware individual grounded in the cosmos commits himself to value life and serenity as the foundation of personality. Gathered from many sources and disciplines, it becomes increasingly clear that creating and sustaining life reflects the basic intention of the universe. Integrity means to be an integral part of the universal life force.

Integrity characterizes harmonic relations between parts of the psyche. Citizens no longer passive and indifferent reflect an unimpaired condition of integration of both short and long term motivations. It becomes a code of personal honor. They are willing to bear consequences of their convictions in the face of scorn and threat. People of integrity, having made their commitments, hold true to them.

Personal integrity includes proper regard for community values, ends, and goals. Citizens have a sure grasp of moral obligations and willingly pay the price for their allegiance. This reduces their willingness to judge others and supposes a vast world of possibilities within which to agree and disagree, resist and reconcile, to harm and heal. A fanatic can't change his mind and won't change the subject. Fanatics lack respect for considerations, values, and deliberations of others. In their willingness to do harm terrorist nullify the fundamental integrity of the cosmos, themselves, and the community.

Natural Law

We do not know where natural law comes from or its provenance. Like so many things in the universe law emerges from a world beyond our imagination. Whether you believe it or not the Law of Gravity works immediately and continuously. The Law of Singularity also works continuously, but because of immensity of the universe its effects take longer to discern. Einstein in a famous reflection said: "the most incomprehensible thing about the universe is that it is comprehensible." The universe itself is source of meaning. Natural Law more than merely describing reality reports its function. Our work as humans is to state our hypotheses of physical and metaphysical laws and by observation and deduction test them for reality. Physics and metaphysics come together in provocative and haunting ways. Clearly the universe is much larger and more dynamic than we imagined.

For reasons we don't understand the physicists Double Slit Experiment demonstrates that the most fundamental particles and waves of the universe appear and disappear. Why and where they go we can only imagine. It is no surprise at the present state of evolution much is unknown about metaphysical law. The intuitive knows his relation to fundamental being and spends time on the pathless path. This represents our best effort to ascertain dignity and destiny of human existence.

Despite human intention to state what is fundamental in the universe, law is a dynamic idea modified through time, study, and experience. Laws depend on the degree of understanding and usefulness humans are able to achieve at their moment in history. When a faulty Law is identified it is consciously changed to produce a more congruent and useful action. While we do not have a meta-law designed to explain the change process. It is enough to see contingency in the matter.

Principles Of Personal Integrity

Principles are down stream representations of natural law. The Law of Singularity states everything in the universe is related to everything else as an internally consistent solitary unit. The cosmos is an orderly, harmonious whole composed of non-tangible energy and meaning. That which lies beyond mass is metaphysical or in the strict sense of the word supernatural. To live by principle is to choose that which grounds personal being and thinking. On an ordinary day principles are landmarks on the road to integrity. When facing life challenges that which before was merely potential can be reified and influence matters. The practice of spiritual religion grows soul, and strengthens the moral fiber of the individual.

Each individual as part of the whole is responsible for his fate and that part of the social fabric into which he was born. To fulfill our destiny and achieve our highest ideals we must rethink who we are and what we are about. To do this we first must establish principles that source and organize thought. Principles are intrinsic qualities or elements that determine the nature of thought and consequent behavior. They are laws governing natural phenomena or mechanical processes. According to Christian Scientists a principle reveals the mind of God. Principles are a matter of discovery and co-creation. They exist as given. Human destiny is to make them real.

Those of us in the Western tradition argue we must discipline and organize ourselves to solve practical problems in order to pursue metaphysical goals. The Eastern tradition argues our primary life effort is to seek wholeness of being. Whatever comes of that is fate. *Fiat Justitia ruat coelum*. (Bring forth justice though the heavens fall). In either case by maintaining consciousness we extrapolate principles in order to share both mediated and unmediated knowledge and work to make the globe habitable for everyone.

If an individual chooses to live by principle he will strive to be transparent and honest in his dealings with others. Aware of the frailty of human reason he will withhold judgment, see beyond the moment, learn by trial and error. Practicing spiritual religion he achieves inner spaciousness called soul through which transcendent energy flows. For the enlightened, violence becomes an unacceptable substitute for problem-solving. He will accept less in the presence of more and daily create opportunities to care for those presented to him by fate. Larger goals are ending violence establishing demographic balance, expanding reach of science, and meeting basic needs of individuals for food, shelter, work, education, medical care.

Levels Of Consciousness

William James book [17] postulated an individual has four levels of consciousness. Baba Muktananda saw in the human being four bodies stacked within the other; physical, subtle, causal, and supracausal. Each gives rise to amazing experiences. [18] Each level or state can be further delineated into subtle structures or personalities. In the outline below two are combined.

---

[17]   Principles of Psychology 1890.
[18]   The Secret of the Siddhas #83 1980

Physical body Physical brain generates awakened state "Sensorial attention"
Subtle Body Preconscious mind generates thought and dream state "Passive attention"
Causal body Witness consciousness give rise to awareness and deep sleep "Steady attention of the mature mind"
Supracausal body Pure consciousness is experience of the transcendent now "Awareness of awareness"

Awareness plus understanding of the structure and function of mind, in James words, removes "the gray chaotic indiscriminateness of people who are incapable of paying attention." Discovery of the dynamics of self reveals fundamental knowledge of the cosmos. Light, truth, and peace exists in us all. To love another is honoring who we and who they are.

All People Are Of Inestimable Value

Given obvious differences among people, arguing all sentient life has equal value, appears a radical assertion. It is our first principle. Political theories with this assumption are scorned as utopian. Power and wealth are thought to be measures of individual value. Not only do these increase human misery, with the rise of military technology they threaten existence of life on the planet. Lord Acton said the obvious "power tends to corrupt and absolute power corrupts absolutely." [19]

---

[19]   Letter to Bishop Creighton 1887

Calm Abiding, Mindfully Growing Soul

The fully conscious individual decides to live simply, with childlike directness, and inner transparency. A catalogue of behaviors of the wise includes:

- Absence of artifice, wiles and duplicity.
- Quiet and serene attitude.
- Rational/emotive transparency
- Acceptance of others pain.
- Unwillingness to mask feelings.
- Sincerity and lack of pretention.
- Freedom from self disgust.
- Absence of deceit and treachery.
- Love without dissimulation

Forming the social enterprise around inner directed values of the common man earns scorn from the practical as too credulous. Critics contend dreamers impede functioning of the practical world. Visionaries are heroes we garland with our highest honors. Who dare say the ingenuous are not models for a new world?

Wholeness

It is a law governing natural phenomenon the world is not two of anything. Our brains are composed of matter and anti-matter find this difficult to comprehend. Bilateral brains reflect the duality of existence. Ego builds into thought and language our separation from one another. That I am not you appears the most common of senses.

Look deeper and see we all share same consciousness. To mend the fabric of existence we must be clear about interdependence of all living things. Confidence in the wholeness and perfection of all things is our source of insight and courage.

Sanctity Of Life

When we hallow life and deem it holy, we stand at the threshold of understanding our true nature. Those who have crossed to awareness have first hand knowledge that life is sacrosanct and everyday precious. All individuals have transcendent moments in which they surmise their greatness and destiny. Some will never see the light and wantonly destroy themselves and others. Sympathy for those who live in darkness is based on the surety they will have occasion to right the wrong they did. The inviolability of cause and effect argues they will have Karmic opportunities to align with the intention of the universe to cherish life.

Children Our Joy

William Wordsworth reflecting on the joy of childhood set the standard pretty high.

> Our birth is but a sleep and a forgetting:
> The soul that rises with us, our life's star,
>   Hath had elsewhere its setting,
>   And cometh from afar:
> Not in entire forgetfulness,
> And not in entire nakedness,
> But trailing clouds of glory do we come
> From God, who is our home.[20]

In the surprise and joy of new born innocence and purity, humans sense their elegance and greatness. The ingenuous child ego state, with bright and hopeful feelings and hidden potential, is the most precious part of us at any age. All children deserve education in hard and soft sciences, literature, lore, and arts of their people. Knowledge strengthens human bonding and reduces potential for violent conflict.

---

[20]   Intimations of Immortality From Recollections of Early Childhood V5

Above All Do No Harm

The interrelation of principles speaks to their universal character. What is true at one tier of analysis cascades through all other levels. It is fundamental that one cannot be enlightened and harm others. Built into the warp and woof of reality is the sagacity "above all do no harm." Bringing about peace on earth, demands that we refocus our attention from outer to inner dynamics, and create society based, not on tortured reason, but on our deepest and dearest vision of ourselves, our forefathers, and love for those who will succeed us.

Create Justice At All Costs

To espouse justice in complex social settings often creates a no-win situation. The illumined facing possible failure can not be persuaded to abandon the cause, while the fanatic is driven by unseen forces. The motto of Justice John Marshall [21] F*iat Justitia pereat mundus* tells the truth we seek. If we abandon principle we surrender that which defines and creates high destiny.

> The destiny of mankind is not decided by material computation. When great causes are on the move in the world...we learn we are spirits not animals, and that something is going on in space and time, and beyond space and time, which, whether we like it or not, spells duty.[22]

Honor

Everything is not relative. Some things stand as foundation of both objective and subjective reality. The quality of honor, or unimpaired soundness via principles is grounded in the nature of things. There is a place inside individuals they can trust which calls forth justice and compassion. While vagaries of circumstance and difficulties of language give honor a gossamer quality, it cannot be gainsaid, deep down desire within all beings is desire for meaning and peaceful coexistence.

---

[21] Let Justice Prevail And The World Perish
[22] Winston Churchill, The university of Rochester New York 1941

Complex Problems.

The role of personal integrity is crucial to solving the large, multi-faceted inter-national problems. When you enter the maize of complex problems the life force points the direction and guides the person of integrity. With careful reflection a pathway is provided. At the same time we are not prevented from failing in our efforts. Failure can become a stimulus to greater effort. Churchill reminded his countrymen: "you will make all kinds of mistakes; but as long as you are generous and true, and also fierce, you cannot hurt the world or even seriously distress her. She was made to be wooed and won by youth."[23] It becomes a matter of learning and adjusting that gives meaning to our lives. At one level Jesus was powerful and convincing. At another he tasted the bitterness of failure. Like Mother Theresa who many times wondered out loud why God had abandoned her.

Parameters of Possible Action.

Situations focus our attention, define problems to be faced including possible courses of action. The responsible individual ask questions as he seeks to reduce complexities to solvable dimensions

Where do I enter?
What resources do I bring to the matter
What do I resist?
With whom do I team?
How do I build trust?
How do I make my values clear?
What is the cost benefit of intermediate conflicts?
What measurements must be kept?
What battles are not worth winning?
What price will I not pay?
How do I expand time for reflection and research?
How do I avoid distractions deliberate or unconscious?

23

What is the most effective order for unraveling complexities?
What is the role of vision and how do I achieve it?
What risk is worth the cost?
Can personal sacrifice contribute to achieving outcome?

Quantum Insight

A humane philosophy will include space/time dimensions of the universe. If we are going ferret out order and meaning let us face the possibility that the search will brings us face to face with an unknown universe in which order and value are elusive. The Questions we face are challenging, but at the same time Quantum Mechanics reveals knowledge that echoes scholars musings for thousands of years. Counter-intuitive revelations are reflections for re-grounding meaning and rethinking fragile rationality.

Demography

Maintaining balance and avoiding extremes is a fundamental principle. Creation demands a state of equilibrium. To keep human population in parity with planetary resources sufficient to maintain it, we must gather data, formulate hypothesis, develop plans, and draw common conclusions. Not an easy business. Nevertheless with proper education most people will understand the cost/benefit and willingly participate in maintaining demographic balance.

Money As Means Not Ends

Money is a means not an end of social enterprise. This is a fundamental remake of human motivation which appears only able to value what it can seen and touch. Fundamental mathematical equations are not true in themselves but reflect a larger reality. Spiritual reality has the same feature. To decide a persons value by the size of his portfolio is impertinent to the human enterprise. To accept less in the presence of more reflects re-alignment of social values in a way that might contribute to social betterment.

Hypocrisy

Lord Acton in 1881:"There is no error so monstrous that if fails to find defenders…."[24]One of the most distressing sights of social miasma is denial of the obvious. When put in the service of power, myth, and injustice reasons can be used to create ideological monsters. Add a little hocus-pocus, waving banners, and marching bands whole nations comes under sway of phantasms of hypocrisy. You might think the enormity of the lie would expose itself on the grounds no one would lie about something so large. To some the bigger the lie the bigger the acceptance.

Self Sustaining Communities

Humans are social animals. The technical world conspires against creating dynamic social entities. Particularly painful to watch is children attached to a vast array of inhuman electronic equipment substituting for personal encounter. Under duress of electronic games and diversions public educations fails our children and families. A small self-sustaining society of honorable individuals based on life cycle and drama of the seasons is a model which enriches the heart and soul.

Eschew Vengeance

Evil for evil slaying, without due process of law is retaliation. If an individual lacks self-control and responds retributively to anger, integrity is abandoned and the social fabric torn. If hostility is allowed to escalate to lawlessness and riot the human enterprise is degraded. When massive slaughter tears the fabric of society, innocents suffer dire consequences, and citizens shrink in fear. At times we are called on to surrender self-concerns to further life for the less fortunate.

Ego Mind

Many people suffer feelings of inadequacy. This is the source of arrogance that motivates individuals to prove themselves superior to others. Discussion often has an Alice in Wonderland aspect, "if I say

---

24   Lord 'Acton letter to Mary Gladstone in 1881

a thing three times it is true. I do not think error." Ego mind projects certainty when tentativeness might suggest viable differences to be heard and considered. Assertion of the ego is sometimes accompanied by a drive to diminish others.

Faulty reasoning often spirals downward into heightened conflict. The alert individual is continuously aware of that part of himself not governed by his or others anger. He finds himself able to create a quiet and serene place from which to observe his own and others thinking. He is able to see past the immediate to where higher possibilities appear for consideration and action.

When this higher self is active his desire to harm others has no traction. Seeking first the ground of being he works to further justice and compassion. For the person of integrity this is no choice. He is in a process of constant rebirthing, reawakening to possibilities outside ordinary thought patterns.

The purpose of life is to strengthen alignment with the intention of the universe to create and maintain life. His work is to make clear within himself and the other the necessity of a pacific attitude.

Positioned between higher and lower promptings, the observer faces the choice between ego power or attunement with the principles of life. Choice of the lesser self often has grim consequences. The higher self comes with obstacles of its own. Either path presents obstructions and impediments that take the measure of the individual. Higher consciousness is the constant mentor for justice and compassion. In choosing to work for human betterment and peace among institutions, communities, and nations, the individual becomes co-creator of the universe.

Feeling

Feeling is a psychic state composed of emotions, sentiments, and desires. It produces an affective state of complementary pictures, sounds, and bodily sensations. Instinctive emotions are involuntarily built into the physiology of the individual. They include fear, anger, lust and generosity. Sexual craving passing as love adds drama to the human encounter while insuring survival of the species. Primitive emotions are often intense and irrational. Unmodulated feelings accounts for much of the dysfunction in society.

The thoughtful individual is aware of his sentiments and shapes them to human form. Having searched out the range of emotions molds them to the human situation. Love which previously was raw and ungovernable becomes a source of bonding and empowerment. When emotions are under control we designate the individual as judicious and discreet. Having recognized limitations and pitfalls of cognitive thought an aware individual finds himself viewing life from a shifted perspective. That which before was ordinary, now shimmers with transcendence. Into the space of no-mind the life force manifests joy and meaning. The commonplace is illuminated teeming with possibilities beyond thought. Freed from machinations of mortal mind, responding to higher knowledge within, we describe the individual as enlightened.

Depression

In a materialist technological culture with weakening social ties it is not surprising there is a high incidence of emotional depression. When individuation replaces group life, and relationships are valued by their contribution to fiscal realities, families flounder. Individuals bereft of intimacy experience sadness and dejection. Depression is a state marked by the inability to focus attention, reduction of physiological vigor, plus feelings of gloom and hopelessness. When untreated mild neurotic disassociation may descend to a psychotic state which damages individuals intellectual, emotional, and physical health leading to despondency and suicidal impulses.

Other People Don't Cause You

Many people suffer from feelings of inadequacy It is commonplace for individuals to accept themselves on the grounds that other people value them. "If they like me I must be worthwhile," is the rationalization. It is not without reason "birds of a feather flock together. Giving power for your well-being to another unhorses both self and other. On the other hand, mutual interdependency of individuals who share trust and discernment produces a transcendent state of insight, power, and purpose. Maintaining integrity, individuals become channels of healing love and protection for themselves and to those whose care they are committed.

Few mental processes are more destructive of human health and social integration than I am this way because of you. "You make me mad. I can't trust you. I need you to be happy." The person uses the strategy "if it weren't for you I could," to gain acceptance from another and to feel good about himself and obscure his deleterious behavior.

The average person, given what he knows, does best he can with life. Operating out of pre-conscious mind the individual adjusts his life to fit preconceptions, opinions, values, and past events. He makes up reality and invites and/or manipulates others to join him. Events are tallied to prove what he said was true in the first place. In the domain of concept reality often gets lost in the miasma of discussion.

It takes practice to liberate the higher self and have confidence that life is not being done to you. A major benefit of self-awareness is to witness consciousness whereby the person is cognizant of feelings of despair and hopelessness and at the same time is not controlled by them. Steps to neutralize feelings of dejection and re-establish sense of wholeness and happiness include the following diagram:

Establish Witness Consciousness
Enlivening the distinction between mind and Observer is fundamental to establishing, integrity, self-respect, and freedom from other-directed values of a materialist culture.
Be Non-judgmental
Experience self as an autonomous force. With incredible lightness of being you are able to disassociate from preconscious mind to enjoy the irony and humor in life.

Avoid Hostile Situations

Do what is necessary to maintain distance from destructive conflict. When unable to avoid conflict, reach deep into your reservoir of life force to see through the immediate events and summon healing power to the contest.

Reach Out To Those That Love You

Love we receive from family and friends is a gift from the life force. Compassion is always the same in all people everywhere. It is the shared conscience of the universe. When you love your neighbor you are loving yourself.

Establish A Haven Of Peace and Comfort

Create a place for daily meditation and reflection. Over time it will become a space of spiritual amperage. Go there daily to restate your intention and send healing prayers to others.

Keep A Journal

Becoming a person of integrity is not for the casual individual. It takes self-awareness, time, and willingness to learn from mistakes. Keeping a daily journal of discoveries and learning is a major contribution to mindfulness and growth of soul.

Share Learning With Others.

Integrity is being grounded in the principles of a universe that includes all sentient beings. Shared insight contributes to the warp and woof of the universe. Everyone, literally everyone, benefits.

CHAPTER FOUR

LIFE FORCE IS LOVE

The universe is created as a living theater of consciousness manifesting the life force. We are immersed in the drama of life. Matter is evanescent and the universe is a field of energy bearing reverence for life. Intention and prayer brings forth that which was built in from the beginning.

The life force is love. Neither metaphoric nor poetic, this is an existential statement that describes fundamental reality. In another milieu it was averred: "God is love; he who dwells in love dwells in God, and God in him."[25] More than DNA, genealogy, neural networking, brain cortex, and built-in erotic impulses, love is the in flowing and out channeling of life force in human affairs. By its power it enlightens mind, inflames soul, inspires arts, and contains visions for the destiny of the race. It empowers human search for meaning, structure, and design. Those aware seek to make it enduring in human affairs.

It energizes social cohesion, embraces accommodation, seeks the common good, and finds meaning in the surrendering of ego self. Instinctive sex drive guarantees continuation of the race. Surprise and delight in the newborn are primary sources of tenderness and carefulness in human families. Seers disassociated from ordinary society call it bliss and deem it proof of the benignity of the universe. Everyone everywhere is drawn into its orbit.

---

[25]   I John 4:16B

Love is not individual, nor limited by personal considerations. When managing your deeper self you access source energy of creation. Plato was right. By reflection we share perfection built into the universe. As we grow soul, more power is available to reach out to heal others and solve complex problems. To love another because they love you misses the point. Love has no intention or desire for repayment. Consider Jesus biting counsel on the matter. "If you love only those who love you, what reward have you. Even tax collectors do that much."[26] The quality of our thought and that which we intend for others influences reality. We are causative in the matter of compassion and justice. "You shall be perfect as your father in heaven," is how Jesus sees it. Love is energy and beauty rolled into one. Under its influence a man might choose to expend his life for others.

Individuals are structured into and able to be responsible for the entire universe. While individual responsibility is limited by circumstances, a vision of healing and world peace reflects the greatness of the human potential. It is our nature to share the love of God. This is not an overlaid or cultural phenomenon. Self healing, caring for others, and working to mend the fabric of the universe are fundamental activities of the soul. Inspired by the spirit one sees with the eyes of God a world that works for everyone with no one left out.

Consider the opening lines of Genesis: "in the beginning God created the heavens and earth and saw that it was good." Whether looking deep into the human psyche or far out into the cosmos one cannot escape the awesome beauty of creation. Fill your thoughts with the inherent splendor in which you exist every day of your life. There is no error in trusting love. Life force is the law of being, therefore be not afraid. As the life force enters consciousness the individual experiences serenity, dominion, direction, insight, and power. It shows up in human terms as a loving and encouraging voice within accompanied with meaningful images, "can do" feelings and gratitude.

Our daily challenge is to not be distracted by mind considerations and dissuaded by fear. Knowing you have already lived many lifetimes

---

[26]   Matthew 5:46 ff

and will choose to live many more is reassuring. It is comforting to being surrounded by the ambient life force inhabited by loved ones who are not very far away. Acts of violence by the unworthy will be repaid in future lifetimes reduces propensity for aggression. The physical passes. The metaphysical lasts.

> Love never disappears,
> Where would it go?
> I have merely retired to the room next door.
> You and I are the same,
> What we were for each other, we still are.
> Speak to me as you always have,
> Do not use a different tone,
> Do not be sad,
> Continue to rejoice in what pleased us,
> Smile and think of me,
> Life means what it always meant.
>
> Our connection is not severed,
> Why should I be out of your soul,
> If I am out of your sight.
> I will wait for you,
> I am not here,
> Just on the other side of the path.
> You see, all is well.

Life force or soul are part of the innate persona. Visions of fresh possibilities for mankind arise out of the soul. Choosing to act justly, rather than being indifferent to the plight of others, manifests the life force. Time and space disappear. Death looses its suasion.

Love is much larger than personal. The life force is reduced to mere character quirk if you deem love private. "Love your enemies, pray for them that persecute you,"[27] is Jesus' counter-intuitive teaching, do good to them that hate you, bespeaks the fundamental nature of the universe. When we understand love is both the means and ends

---

[27]   Matthew 5:44

of life, we are free to care for others and work in their behalf with no aim for reward. There is liberation and joy and in being generous for its own sake.

> Love is not personal,
> It's energy gives life meaning.
> It is beauty, charm of music, dance, and plastic arts.
> Joy of friends,
> Enthusiasms of community.
> Verve and buzz of woods and stream,
> It is bloom of flowers
> Teaching birds to fly.
> Mothers birthing joy suckling newborn
> Shining eyes children.
> It harmonizes and weds male and female
> Infuses life and work
> Vitalizes biosphere
> Ever present spirit
> Endless.
>
> Reason to counsel love toward the hideous,
> Grimace for the ugly and grotesque.
> Patience counsels grandparent,
> Stay the course,
> Endure hardship,
> This too shall pass away.
> Loving neighbor begins to make sense,
> Justice and compassion for those lacking empathy,
> Glimmers to those darkened by vengeance,

Ironically pain and loss prove invaluable to soul growth. "While I hope never to have to go through that much affliction and stress again, at the same time the experience has taught me much," is the sardonic testimony of the enlightened. Light is wrenched from darkness. Working in behalf of others, unwilling to return wrong for wrong, on the stage of life we act out that to which we are called as children of the most high. Love comes from a different place. It is a field that surrounds us.

Understand this
That which you seek is seeking you
When you find it your will identify yourself
Don't be surprised

The place you seek is already inside of you
When you get there you will be home
It is not far

Life force brings it all together-all of it
Meaning, music, beauty, destiny, dance
All sacred effort

If you look carefully you will see
Things are perfect just the way they are
There is no other possibility

The Life Force infuses all aspects of the universe. Every subatomic particle, cell and fiber of the biobody, every field in deep space.

LIFE FORCE OF THE UNIVERSE.

UNDISCOVERED SYMMETRIES OF SPACE/TIME
9. Physical and Metaphysical science.

WAVE/PARTICLE DUALITY
8. We create reality

WITNESS CONSCIOUSNESS
7. Observer is not changed by what it knows and experiences.

MIND PARADIGMS
6. Five ego states, five representational systems, four polarities.

PERSONALITY COMPOSITION
5. Birthing, parenting, acculturation, assimilation

INSTINCTS
4. Food, sleep, sex, fear, anger, altruism, language facial recognition

---

METAPHYSICAL LAWS
3. Singularity, Entanglement, Perfection, Attraction

AMBIENT FIELD OF CONSCIOUSNESS
2. Humans are fields of energy

LIFE FORCE IS ENERGY
1. There is no vacuum

Diagram Notes

9. Physicists probing ions in the Large Hadron Collider seek as yet unknown forces and symmetries of nature. Astronomers peering deep into space suppose the universe to be composed of unimaginable energy with a minutiae of matter. Working around the edges of cosmic matter in their ranging over metaphysical space the aware find powerful spiritual energies to be source of the *divina mysterium.*

8. The sub-microscopic world of wave/particle duality gives us a clue to the true nature of the universe. The universe is composed of fields of influence radiating waves of energy. At any point in time, the universe presents an array of infinite possibilities. The physical world only comes into being when you focus your attention on it. When you decide what to do next, only then does the future take form out of a vast sea of potential.

7. Self-awareness plus openness to uncover new insights brings about an altered state of mind in which the observer is not changed by what is knows and experiences. Positivism, materialism, and cynicism, are replaced by accession to fields of creative energy. Whereas, before sense perceptions were only basis of knowledge, the enlightened individual perceives dynamics of consciousness as the implicate order of the universe. From this shifted paradigm the individual does not

accept within himself and others rationalizing malignant acts. Not limited to retro-mind, able to envision larger possibilities, the seeker dreams of what could be.

6. A number of approaches have been developed to map structure and function of personality. Examples include Five Ego States of Transactional Analysis, Karl Jung's four Polarities, Sigmund Freud's Theory of the Unconscious, Five Representational Systems of Neuro-linguistic Programming, and Abraham Maslow's Hierarchy of Needs. These are helpful to those seeking liberation from impulsive and compulsive behavior, and desire to rise above instinct to achieve high level outcomes in their lives. Using mind to transcend mind leads to personal integrity and morality.

5. Personality is the accumulated qualities and behaviors instilled in a human being from infancy. Due to radical dependency during childhood, parents character and attitudes are assimilated into living tissue. Through rearing the child adopts customs and attitudes of the prevailing culture.Assigning traits to genetic structure does not obviate the role of parents perspective, and volition.

4. Sensate life comes into being coded with instincts. Built into flesh and immutable they include urge for food, sleep, anger, fear, sex, facial recognition, and language. Intra-uterine life, birthing, parenting and radically dependent childhood creates foundation of the historical document of preconscious mind. We have no direct knowledge of the source of our thinking. What we think about is not caused by what we think about. Thinking arises from this hidden structure.

3. Energy accomplishes things. Metaphysical laws of Singularity, Entanglement, Perfection, and Attraction are built into the universe. Within its deepest places they reflect order in the cosmos with the observer allies individual thinking and behavior. In this we are called to be worthy of our ancestors and future generations.

2. Consciousness is the ambient field of energy surrounding planetary life. Nothing occurs beyond its reach. Sometimes called divine mind, consciousness touches down and inheres within every living entity.

As physicists seek mathematical sense, the aware pursue meaning within the psyche.

1. There is no vacuum. Like space wherein they wander, humans are composed of energy. We are immaterial beings. That which was not born cannot die. It is inescapable, matter is illusory. Loosen the hold of those who say sense perceptions are the only basis of human knowledge and worthwhile thought, and begin to look with quiet eyes and see the aura we call holy surrounding animate life. Become a visionary and see beyond the ordinary.

A new world anthropology must include all aspects of life: space, mortality, apocalyptic events, historical renditions, and limited vision. To be considered serious, our thinking must include all life and be pressed and formed in every moment by ambient consciousness. Calm the body, quiet the mind, open the heart and the spirit will do the work.

Loving kindness is one of the four foundational practices taught by Buddha as transcendent abodes. Others are compassion, sympathetic joy, and equanimity. Loving kindness must include the self. If the instrument is out of tune its tones will be awkward and distorted when played amongst others. Love reflections ingests and abides in kind and generous thoughts and feelings.

Compassion is a healing energy, a manifestation of our consciousness that surrounds the entirety of sentient life. You exist in an ambient field of love. Your soul desires nothing more than to love and be loved. It is not a matter of good behavior or earning reward. You are loved without being worthy or deserving due to your effort. Birthing is an act of love. The intent of creation is support life and love.

Life Force Reflections

Visualize someone who loves you today or loved you unconditionally in the past including parents and family figures. Imagine being in their embrace, listen to their loving tone of voice, and feel their consoling energy. Use your imagination to fill in the emotional content you observe in others but have not experienced yourself.

Give yourself over to feelings and bodily sensations of love that friends and family have accorded you. Realize you are surrounded by a benevolent field of consciousness. You are loved just the way you are. Your job is to access and lathe in it. Evoke and allow yourself to bask and be cradled in the mother love of God.

Stand guard at the doorway of your mind. Disregard negative energy, anger, or fearful feelings arising out of background trauma have no mind on them. They are products of retro-mind; give them no heed. Simply observe them and let them go. Over time they will disappear.

Be prepared for a shift in perspective. When you change the way you look at things, the things you look at change. It takes time to get used to an altered state. Things you thought were permanent recede and that which previously appeared invisible takes on a new life.

If retro-mind persists, interpose quiet prayers. Hear them whispered by the beauty, simplicity, and elegance of nature. Allow your whole being to bathe in this benevolent field of love,

> May all beings be happy
> May all experience comfort of friends and family
> May all be a source of healing for neighbors
> May all escape harm and poor health
> May all die quietly in arms of family

When feeling sad and depressed, bored by banality of daily chores, create for yourself a store house of uplifting sayings that bring both relief and comfort. Memorize and make them part of your heart. Full of consolation let it comfort you:

> The Lord is my shepherd: I shall not want.
> He makes me lie down in green pastures
> He leads me beside still waters
> He restores my soul.
> He leads me in the paths of righteousness
> For his names sake.
> Yea though I walk through the valley of the shadow of death
> I will fear no evil for thou art with me,
> Thy rod and staff comfort me.
> Thou prepares a table for me in the presence of my enemies,
> Thou anoints my head with oil,
> My cup runs over.
> Surely goodness and mercy shall follow me
> All the days of my life,
> And I will dwell in the house of the Lord forever.[28]

---

28 Psalm 23

CHAPTER FIVE

THE SIMPLEST TRUTH

The simplest truth is individuals are responsible for their own physical and mental health. They have duty to care for family, consider their neighbors, serve the country, and green the earth. Not overlaid or incidental these moral faculties are built into human consciousness. Not the purview of an elect few but the endowment of the entire race. In any age when speaking of the rebirthing of the nation the intention is to clarify fundamental principles and expand the public conscience.

Success and failure at different stages in the life cycle are part of the grand design to teach simple truths. Trees having lost their leaves in the Fall do not lament their poverty. Roses blooming in the Spring do not boast their beauty. What goes around, comes around. Ups and downs back and forth are all part of the drama of the evolution of human consciousness.

Television is the nemesis of those seeking to expand their inner core and grow the soul of the nation. The media pumps amnesia into citizens living room that encourages the denial of reality. Limited to mercantile considerations and pandering to the instinctive part of the human psyche, producers pimp violence, sex, and the worst human features. Dominant and recurring themes embossed on the minds of citizens include:

Only money and power matter
Morality is for those who can't compete
We make history. Others talk about it.
Every day may be your last. Make the most of it.
Nursing home is for the old folks
Violence is the heartbeat of entertainment
Sex is marketable
Take all you can get
Greed is good
The Rubes will never catch on

One can see the dysfunction built into a society espousing hostile values can go only in one direction and that is downward. In the virtual reality promoted by those wielding power, the rich get richer and the poor pooer.

When the imbalance becomes severe, it is only a matter of time before correction sets in often in the form of riot and revolution.

When the stock market bubble, built on ersatz values, and the credit boom collapsed it brought down the banking system. Billions of dollars of federal money poured into the system will not help absent a sea change of human. values throughout the system. With the unemployment rate over 10%, housing prices off 30%, and the credit market defunct, GNP stands for Gross National Product and Gross National Psychology. Both depressed. Indeed the whole economic world is in a slump.

There is no necessary correlation between rank in organization and competency. Caught up in the frenzy of the moment, leaders on top and associates down the line get caught up in events. Things make sense which on a better day no one would own up to. "Everyone was doing it," is the rationalization for economic madness. A Ponzi landscape is created that gathers in the players, informs their thinking, and leads to a bitter end. To the whistle-blowers question "didn't anyone understand things were absurd" and that crimes were being committed the answer comes back: "everyone was doing it." Individuals were caught up in the game, had neither an alternative to offer nor power to stem the tide. The self-blinded rode the horse over the cliff.

Our institutions are based on the moral responsibility of the individual. It assumes those in control exchange real value and live with the consequences of their decisions. This assumes chief executives have their focus on larger matters, weigh cost/benefits carefully, and abstain from self-indulgence.

The size and complexity of problems our country faces are mind numbing. Where does a responsible person begin? The role of personal integrity is crucial to solving the large, multi-faceted intercontinental problems. When you enter the maize of complex problems the life force points the direction and guides the person of integrity. With careful reflection a pathway is provided. At the same time we are not prevented from failing in our efforts. Failure can become a stimulus to greater effort.

Churchill reminded his countrymen: "you will make all kinds of mistakes; but as long as you are generous and true, and also fierce, you cannot hurt the world or even seriously distress her. She was made to be wooed and won by Youth"[29]. At one level Jesus was powerful and convincing. At another he tasted the bitterness of failure and like Mother Theresa who many times wondered out loud why God had abandoned her.

Situations focus our attention, define problems to be faced including possible courses of action. The responsible individual questions himself as he seeks to reduce large complexities to solvable dimensions, reduce opposition, establish a course of measurable action, and build an operative program.

Where do I enter the problem
What resources do I bring to the table
What professional resources are available
With whom do I team
How do I build trust

---

[29]   Winston Churchill <u>While England Slept</u> 1939

How do I make operational values clear
What is the cost benefit of intermediate conflicts
What measurements would be worth graphing
What battles are not worth winning
What price is too high for a concession
How do I find time for reflection and research
How do I avoid distractions
What is the most effective order of unraveling complexities
What is the role of vision. And how do I achieve it
What risk is worth the cost
What am I willing to tolerate

Solipsism

Personality is created by random events. A psyche, is an assemblage of feelings, positions, images, and attitudes gathered along the way. In an haphazard aggregation we can anticipate neurotic disorder of insecurity, anxiety, depression and irrational fear. Most people suffer feelings or inadequacy and willingly yield control of their minds to external authorities and amusements. For worldly self the only believable reality that can be known and verified is me. Such are closed to possibilities not contained in what they already know. What goes around comes around.

To avoid individual responsibility people agglomerate in self-sustaining communities. Whatever their place or destiny portends, motivated by survival, individuals draw close to neighbors, mother earth, and feral creatures. In celebration of life, hideous past events are remembered with chagrin and their victims objects of continuous prayer. Pyramids in the desert, castles above the Rhine, and skyscrapers on Fifth Avenue become monuments to past vanities

It is necessary to confront the distinction between physical mind and metaphysical energy. In the small white Synagogue in Capernaum on shore of the Sea of Galilee, to the amazement of those watching, Jesus drove a clairaudient demon out of a frenzied man. Scribes and Pharisees observing his power were amazed. What is this new teaching? Whence this authority that spirits obey him?[30] Spiritual practice of Torah equipped him with metaphysical power so he could replace demonic energy with divine. His proximity to the Fathers healing energy built into the structure of the universe enabled him to channel healing. Neighbors saw this as something way beyond their ken. They had no way of seeing a human as a regent of God.

It is not esoteric knowledge secret or otherwise that heals. It is energy. There is a gap between concept and the power of the life force. It is the divide between the unknowable underpinnings of physical life and what we say about it. Not to see and manage this space is to under power our destiny. It's one thing to obsess and keep your story going, it is another to channel healing energy to those around you. To be a regent for the Almighty one learns to stand guard at the door of mind and avoid distractions. Moment by moment the evolved master detaches from the daily and experiences clairvoyance and clairaudience.

Imagination can bring us in contact with insight greater than is knowable by our everyday minds. As St. Paul said "We look not at things that are seen, but at things which are not seen; for the things which are seen are temporal; but the things which are not seen are eternal."[31] Both auditory and imaginings play a critical role in accessing fundamental reality. Imagination must be managed lest it take the form of daydreaming or distracting thought.

Individuals of integrity receive insights not available to mortal mind. Due to its non-sensory derivation, such knowledge is deemed secret and declared gnostic, gospel or spiritual. Grounded in the foundation of the universe, through the practice of silence and serenity, masters receive intuitions from the unknowable. They channel ineffable promptings to create previously unimaginable possibilities. They choose to live transparent and virtuous lives. Moment by moment they manage their minds to free themselves from destructive levels of deceit, greed, and power. Material considerations fade away. Life and

---

[30]   Mark 1:22-28
[31]   II Cor 4:18

51

death distinction disappears. They become inspirations for those they touch and substantive in supporting community organizations.

Often arising without the individuals awareness, the liberated intra-psychic observer allows individuals to perceive machinations of their minds as they happen. This is a break through experience. Mindful of what is going on they are able to detach from memory, interpose alternatives, and daily choose their course. Less at the effect of powerful leaders and bygone days, they enter a continuously aware state of calm abiding. Here they increasingly disassociate from the world of fad and fashion. In deep sleep they access and re-integrate their personalities around their inner selves. Twofold sources of knowledge flows into the evolving master; their native genius as fundamental part of creation plus intuitions and visions from the field of consciousness.

Awakened to the universal order individual consciousness is transformed. From an internal orientation, the enlightened experience the distress and pain of those with lesser opportunities in life. Receding from importance matter depolarizes birthing and dying. Both are expressions of the elan vital. Desire for the good spreads by its own power. Individual effort attracts deep self of others and becomes social and institutional.

Ludwig Wittgenstein

The search for meaning is full of irony. Just when you obtain confidence in your position something shows up refuting your ideas and throwing you back into the conundrum. Three questions provoke us. Is there meaning? If there is how would we know it? What are the implications of our findings for life on the planet?

Another way of approaching the fundamental question was formulated by Ludwig Wittgenstein (1889-1951) in his famous treatise [32] argues problems arise because of the misunderstanding the logic of language. Statements or propositions represent an abstract or mental form of reality termed virtual. Pictures of the physical represent a reality no

---

[32]   <u>Tractatus Logicus Philosophicus</u> 1922

larger than themselves. All propositions say nothing. You cannot represent facts. Whatever you say about them is twice removed first in the mental representation and secondly what you say about it. The limit of language is the border of the knowable world. "What we cannot speak about, we must pass over in silence," commented the Austrian philosopher.

The positivists argue the physical and our sensory appropriation of it is the only reality. Look no further. There is no other. Wittgenstein claimed to have solved the major problems in philosophy. Perhaps he meant by this to quote TS Eliot: "this is the way the world ends, the world ends, the world ends, not with a bang but a whimper."[33] Don't look elsewhere for meaning. What you see is what your get. Beyond sense perception there is nothing. Wittgenstein's most famous quote says this. "The world is all that is the case." How little is achieved when the problems of language are solved.

Wittgenstein sought moral and philosophical perfection in his life. Born to an extraordinarily wealthy and morbid Austrian family, three of four brothers committed suicide. Husbands of two of three surviving daughters went insane. One took his own life. In search for meaning Ludwig sought the simple and secluded life in out-of the way places in rural Austria, Norway, and Ireland. He gave a way a sizeable inheritance. Death is not an event in life, we do not live to experience death. If we take eternity to mean not infinite temporal duration but timelessness, the eternal life belongs to those that live in the present, he advised. To give the essence of a proposition means to give essence of all description the thus the essence of the world. What we are left with is to accept and endure.

Become scientists to our lives.

Humans have ways of knowing that are independent of their sensory organs. They are able to have direct insight into the workings of the universe, and they have direct influence on reality. They learn observe, innovate, and create the consequence of metaphysical insight. Anyone can use paranormal ability to see distant locations.

---

[33]   T.S.Eliot Journey Of The Magi 1927

The Observer

By using mild disassociation some humans are able to objectively view their own psychodynamics and choose outcomes they want for themselves. The observer's outlook reflects the highest values the individual can be aware. The individuals perceptive apparatus shifts from physical to metaphysical through meditation. By practicing serene quietude they receive insight and promptings from the source of creation. By the quality of positive healing energy they know they exist and operate within the universal field of consciousness.

Remote Viewing

Physicists cannot, without expressions of wry chagrin, explain their finding that a single object can be in two places at the same time. They wag their heads in disbelief when they demonstrate, even at great distances, when you stimulate one object you immediately influence the other. Over the centuries seers like Madam Blavaksky, founder of Theosophy, have reported incidences of remote viewing. In our day a mountain of research on the phenomenon has proven that individuals with extra-sensory perception have ability to view objects and persons at a distance. This is another piece of the puzzle outlining the emergence of psychic functioning and a new dimensions of metaphysical anthropology.

Creating By Intention

Things around you don't exist until you pay attention to them. The world is not out there independent of our experience. All things are possible moments of consciousness; moment to moment we choose to bring experience into being. Physicist Werner Heisenberg made clear atoms are not things; they are only tendencies. Instead of seeing and thinking things exist apart from perception begin to intuit the limitless possibilities of the universe that lie beyond our comprehension. Scripture alludes to this emanation.

> The Lord came down to see the city and the tower which mortal man had built. He said "here they are one people with a single language…. Henceforth

nothing they have a mind to do will be beyond their reach." [34]

We humans have ways to access the spiritual part of the brain and connect to the universe at a fundamental level. Our purpose in life is to by intention create fresh possibilities and fill space with mansions of self. To understand our connection to reality is to create increased meaning for ourselves and the world.

When we develop the gift of intentionality we become creators of the good. Let us learn to use our mind to transcend mind, to access the life force, and as channels, bring into being justice and compassion. Walking on the pathless path, we must obviate considerations of mind that mislead us to loose track of ourselves and our true identity.

<u>Create Your Day By Intention</u>
- Write your intentions for the day.
- Ask Observer for a sign so you can't doubt the source.
- When surprised rejoice in gratitude.

Prayer

Down through history human distress matched by human concern sparked petition. Aware of confusion, pain, and loss, moved by pity, prayer is employed to assuage distress. When powered by spiritual energies, not mere factual knowledge, invocation produces beneficial results.

---

[34] Genesis 11:5-6

CHAPTER SIX

THE REACH OF THE HUMAN MIND

Energy is the most fundamental nature of reality. It composes 96% of everything. The underpinning of the universe is energy that responds to coherence. Creating meaning places the human endeavor at the very center of the universe. All matter lies within this ocean of microscopic vibrations referred to by physicists as the Zero Point or Quantum Field, in German 'ganzfeld' meaning 'entirety.' In other places it is referred to as spiritual reality, life force, élan vital or collective unconscious. Everyone and everything in the universe is fundamentally connected to everything else as part of the field.

All that we are or can be exists as part of the ganzfeld. All information comes from the field which holds all knowledge as possibility. Probability is the likelihood a particular even will happen. Statistically probability is the ratio of events that actually happen measured against the total number of possibilities.

All knowledge is contained in the field and can be tapped into, mobilized, and acted upon when necessary. Meditation, observation, and deep dreams increase ability of the individual to receive insight from the field. Savants and genius appear to have easy access. Those reporting memories of past lives and able to contact parallel worlds cannot be dismissed out of hand. The universe is larger and more mysterious than we have imagined. Human rational and emotive processes have to do with information exchange with the field. Higher cognition is interaction between subatomic waves and attention of our minds. We literally resonate with the field. This is key to information processing.

Many paths are available to us at any given moment. Our wishes and intention create our reality. In the creation of meaning human brain power orders the wave pattern of the universe When waves become particles potential becomes actual, order displaces chance, meaning replaces possibility. In all situations the most ordered brain prevails, which is another way to say reason replaces randomness.

We are not collections of isolated individuals. Every part of the universe is in touch with every other part instantaneously. Nonlocality is the ability of electrons to influence each other at a distance without intervening energy. Although it has been demonstrated by contemporary physics, Einstein was uncomfortable with "spooky action at a distance." As essential part of the universe beings cannot be isolated from each other. They share a living system which seeks meaning out of chaos and coherence out of entropy. By observation and gentle intention individuals create their future and mend the fabric of the ganzfeld.

Consciousness is not limited to a single human body, all share the field that informs life. As part of the singularity of all things, individuals have ways of communicating and responding at a distance. At a deep subliminal level people have means of receiving and responding to remote communication even when they are not aware of it. Influence on others by remote communication can be only a bit smaller than influence on oneself.

Focused attention influences our own and other bodies. As we heal ourselves, individuals can project energy into other living beings with positive effect. Research removes all doubts that intention has a powerful measurable effect on all forms of planetary life. Most of us know it as wishful thinking. Humans influence other living things on many levels including muscular and motor, neurological and cellular, wave and particle.

The ability to influence others is a function of the degree of the individuals spiritual development and depth of desire to do good to another. Also the level of need in the other strengthens effectiveness of the effort. Such intervention is a two way street. Other people can have the same effect on you that you have on them. Letting someone express good intention toward you is almost as good as meditating on yourself.

Preconditions for success in remote healing are: a positive attitude and belief in the meaningfulness of planetary life, a sense of the singularity and wholeness of the cosmos, a willingness to accept the unthinkable when it appears, and recognition all individuals have some degree of potential to be influenced and effected by the intention of others.

Alertly tapping into the deep well of the ganzfeld brings about an altered state of consciousness which is precursor to remote communication. Steps necessary to bring this about are well known.

> A positive attitude.
> Belief in the meaningfulness of planetary life.
> Sensory deprivation opens door of access to the field.
> A sense of the singularity and wholeness of the cosmos.
> Quietude and silence replaces sensory and mental activity.
> A willingness to accept the unthinkable when it shows up.
> Experience a sense of solidarity with the distant person.
> Omniscient knowing replaces linear cognition.
> Metaphysical events hove into view including telepathy,
>   synchronicity, remote viewing, distant healing,
>   clairvoyance, clairaudience, and psychokinesis.

There is another side to this coin. Our capacity to make good things happen to others is matched by our power to make bad things happen. Mired in the duality of materialism individuals find reasons for harming others. The absurdity of life is an easy argument to make. In this context self-aggrandizement appears an eminently sensible course of action. The pain we cause others is shrugged off as the cost of doing business. Violence, greed, vengeance and hate are merely means by which the fit survive in what they deem a meaningless existence. Accompanied by a sea of rationalizations life is viewed as a dog eat dog world. Warring against the innocent and enjoying the pain of the helpless are rewards garnered by the powerful. In a state where honor and integrity loose their regency, hate, terrorism, and vengeance are promoted in the name of the motherland, ancient heroes, and providence. In a violent context where the inane appears the only course of action, reason becomes chief of many victims.

The Law of Attraction notes whereas the righteous are charmed by good, evil attracts the malicious. Each of us exists at the core of the intersection between the physical and metaphysical. Daily, even momentarily we must choose between good and evil. Deciding in favor of the material world the individual succumbs to desires and pleasures of the moment. Choosing to pursue the immaterial course the individual opts for life marked by exploring the inner dynamics of the ganzfeld.

Through psychological shielding individuals can block or prevent effects of negative influences flowing in their direction. Interposing positive thoughts in the form of sacred images, uplifting prayers, and ingesting positive feelings shields the individual from penetration by demonic energy.

Discovering the mind is a psychical organ in touch with the entirety of the universe opens the door to a world-wide beneficence. There is a space within each individual, no matter how darkened his mind, that when he comes from it, he can be trusted absolutely to pursue justice and compassion. Creating this space between retro-mind and conscious mind is the intention of the practice of anthroposophy.

Our efforts to create a just, rational and compassionate society are important, precisely because the issue of good and evil on the planet remains undecided. Some argue these are the last days of planet earth before human life destroys itself. Despairing of the outcome some date the apocalypse to the year 2012. The good which seeks to be born in us every minutes calls us to the greatness of our destiny.

CHAPTER SEVEN

ANTHROPOSOPHY

I admire Rudolf Steiner (1861-1925) and join his effort to build a spiritual science with the same precision and clarity a scientific investigator approaches the physical world. Through inner development an individual can obtain an objective, rational, and comprehensive experience of the spirit world. In the generic sense, anthroposophy means wisdom about humanity. It is the name assigned his work and that of his followers. While I align on the means and ends of his movement, I use anthroposophy in its most extensive sense.

A metaphysicians task is not to add to an individuals knowledge nor detract from what is known and believed. Rather it is to transform and raise cognitive knowledge to a higher level. The task is not to look backward to establish truth and reveal error. Rather it is to develop the realization energy is the basis of reality, and matter is illusory. As anthroposophists we enlist individuals to pursue the dreams of the saints of all times who through inner development sought to replace the domain of absurdity and create a peaceable kingdom on planet earth. Movement from the physical to metaphysical is outlined in the diagram and notes below.

PHYSICAL   METAPHYSICAL

PHYSICAL	METAPHYSICAL
1. Linear, physical	Field Theory
2. Non-dynamic revealed certainty	Evolving scientific methodology
3. Concept and agreement	Energy transmission
4. Solipsistic reason	Clairvoyance, clairaudience
5. Newtonian cause-and-effect	Quantum nonlocality
6. Space/time limited	Timelessness
7. Other time and place oriented	Singularity "all-at-onceness"
8. Closed system	Open system
9. A posteriori Inductive	A priori Deductive
10. Positivism	Idealism.

1.In the physical world brain and mind are the same. They live and die together in humans. Life has a linear quality. Field theory makes it clear everything is related to everything else. There are no isolated individuals.

2. Certainty, truth, and belief are givens of the brain/mind for which there are no alternatives. The aware use the mind to transcend mind and access the teeming world of unlimited possibility.

3. Concept is a thought or notion formed in the mind. It only knows what it knows and makes sense to itself. Alert awareness makes clear alignment with the fundamental energy and opens a life of previously unknown possibilities.

4. Mind makes sense talking to itself and the like-minded. Thinking in circles, the cat doesn't know the tail is his. On the other hand intuition is receipt of knowledge unmediated by the senses.

5. Cause and effect controls and limits possibilities in the closed Newtonian world. In the Quantum World nonlocality creates a completely dynamic reality of which human consciousness is a basic component.

6. In traditional thought space and time are supposed to be obvious limits of human thought and destiny. Time reversal symmetry

assumes that besides the present, individuals can equally influence the past and future.

7. The human mind stuck in the domain of concept values the past or future more than the present. It is inconceivable everything should happen all at once. And that appears the case. We have much to learn about ourselves.

8. Human life is an analogy for the physical world which presumptively is a closed system with a beginning and an end. When in an altered state we realize we exist in a sea of endless possibilities.

9. Empirical or inductive argument is from the specific to the general. It is a logical process of deriving general principles from particular facts or instances. (A posteriori) On the other hand deductive argument reaches a conclusion by reasoning from the general to the specific, from a known cause to a necessarily related event. An inference is drawn from a general principle. (A priori)

10. Positivists such as Auguste Comte (1798-1857) argue sense perceptions of the physical and derived practical knowledge are the only trustworthy reality. Idealists, on the other hand, insist physical reality is a poor representation of the pure idea and absolute perfection of a thing.

Human motivation and behavior arises out of that part of mind not in our awareness. For this insight mankind will forever be indebted to the Austrian Sigmund Freud (1856-1939). What you are afraid of leads the person deeper into distress. Fear is an instinctive drive. It is a function of the individuals degree of feeling intensity plus passivity to rational processes. Most people are passive to this reality as the following chart suggests.

Subliminal Stimuli	Intermediation	Behavior
Innate drives compel obedience to pre-conscious mind both instinctive and learned.	Ingested media culture, where feeling intensity and rational passivity issue into inane fashionable violence and sex.	Ego-oriented down-ward trending toward disorder and randomness

Talk therapy is helpful when the patient is able to disassociate from instinctive drives, bring mental processes into awareness, observe alternative consequences and choose behaviors that support individual moral and social ethical behavior.. Cf below

Subliminal Stimuli	Intermediation	Behavior
Inborn neurological attitudes, of anger, fear, sexuality, and generosity.	Awareness replaces mental passivity and inserts space into the rational process allowing choice	Rationally adapted moral and ethical behavior aligns with the ganzfeld.

In the era of Quantum Physics things have been turned upside-down. Whereas before science proceeded deductively. Observation of physical facts lead to necessarily related causes. Movement was from the general to the specific. Today physics has uncovered a previously unimaginable super-empirical field of non-locality and proceeds inductively to find explanations for their discovery in the objective world.

Observation of human behavior moving down the steps of consciousness deductively leads to discovery of moral and ethical laws. Inversely moving up the scale inductively we discover a new physical reality.

- Behavior is innate. Individuals mindlessly act out of past positions. They tend to relive historic arguments without awareness of larger implications for the here and now. Human action is instinctive.

- Rationalizations are reasons created to explain what lives only in argument and are not objectively verifiable. Also referred to as "begging the question". Virtual is simulated reality that exists in concept only.

- In a deteriorating situation the individual must determine what course to take and upon what basis the decision made. In colleague with others, he must consider the cost/benefit ratio and what may be the short and long term consequences of his decision.

- Human thinking arises out of preconscious mind and is deductive. We only know what we think after we think it. Put another way, what we are thinking about is not caused by what we are thinking about.

- Finally there is the larger metaphysical drama of the ganzfeld which connects everything to everything else and in which all life appertains. Rather than narrow existence bounded by mortality, we exist in a new world, a cosmos teeming with undreamed of possibilities.

World-wide we face cultural failure. The rule of law is everywhere being eviscerated by those seeking untrammeled power. Violence and sexual depravity are flaunted in all sorts of media. Women's fashions have devolved to the point women are deprived of their sense of dignity and central role amongst us. Despite President Dwight Eisenhower's (1890-1969) warning the military industrial complex continues to be the largest international industrial effort. World-wide caches of lethal armaments threatens institutional life on the planet. Creating a viable anthroposophy is work of all citizens who value life for themselves and succeeding generations.

> God is an energy field,
> Matter is illusory.
> Humans inhere in the ganzfeld,
> We are always and ever children.
> Facial recognition espies God.
> Our green mother nature

Caresses with smell of woods and stream
Whispers affection in flowers, feathers, and fur.

We were born newbies and so we die.
Infant innocence in delivery nurse arms,
Diverts itself for a life distance,
Rests smiling in closed coffin.

Where can we hide from pain of others.
Necessary narcosis dissuades from grief,
Savage portents of mindless pride
Blots out vacant faces of lost children
Us.

Mincing down the walkway a façade of fashion
Striving for a tan of fame in the social sun,
Are moments of certain discovery,
The absurdity of existence.
Of which we are essential.

That's a surprise hard to analyze,
Breathing, fornicating, defecating,
As meaningful anything.
Much less the field of all of it.

Altered state is the parent of new life.
Suspends accusatory guilt,
Accesses the bright field,
Grows tenderness in touch,
Ripens fruitage,
Effloresces flowers.
Sweetens grape.
Makes lithe leap of horn,
Talls stalks of corn.

To make sense out of the senseless,
To see omnisciently all in a moment

One wanders and wonders in mind,
Doubtful of divine caress.
Yet something in mesmerizing quiet
Speaks.
Unseen is viewed,
Unspoken is heard,
Aureole presence palpable to deep knowing,
To those willing to accost silence.
To listen,
Be charmed,
Sneaking delight and hope,
Smiling within the coffin.

How hard to accept this moment,
Without accusations of dire self.
Amid press to flee to distraction
Bring relief to a troubled self.
O sweet Jesus
Cast me not into the world again.
With you mankind is perfected,
Its purpose plain.
Light beckons, darkness dispells
Eternal finger draws pictures of delight
In shifting sands of time.
O sweet savior
Cast me not into the maelstrom again.

CHAPTER EIGHT

MORTAL MIND DIVINE MIND

There are a hundreds names for the vital force of the universe. In the Eastern tradition there is a service reciting a thousand names of God. It includes a variety of designations, titles, values, actions, powers, manifestations and the like. In place of simple ritualistic tribal belief you glimpse the elegance, wondrous depth and complexity of the universe. Here are 120 to start with.

Our Father * Supreme Being * Creator * Sustainer * God Head * Elohim * Baba * Transcendent One * Mediator of Divine Love * Life Force * Allah * Jesus * Torah * Brahman * Atman * Elan Vital * Universal Providence * Immutableness * The Word * Alpha and Omega * Consciousness * The Almighty * Holy Spirit * Deity * Redeemer * Divine Energy * Singularity of all things * Primary Life Force * Vishnu * Beyond Which Nothing * Ruling Spirit * Pathless Path * Efflorescence of flowers * Observer * Buddha Nature * Paramashiva * Eternal Destiny * Perfection of all things * Yahweh * Spaciousness * Omniscient One * Conscience * Eternal Spirit * Sine Qua Non * Salvatore * Perfect Memory * Kundalini Shakti * Absolute * Pure I Am * Bhagawan * Lord Shiva * Chiti * Music of the Spheres * Heavenly Mother * Celestial Being * Celestial Goddess * Effulgence of Nature * Vital Energy * Nirvana * Theosophy * Omnipotent One * Man Upstairs * All Merciful One * Healing Energy of the Universe. * Holy One of Israel * Heartedness * Ruler of the

Universe * Infinite Mind * Supernatural Being * Manifestation of Love * Principle Being * Locum Tenens of Nature * Manifest Destiny * Glorified One * Joy of Being * Source of Bliss * Holiness In All things * Divine Immanence * Great I Am * Holy Ghost * Fullness of Truth * Queen of Heaven * Kingdom of God * Prince of Peace * Ocean Of Love * Intention Of The Universe. * Superposition * Lord of Hosts * Ancient of Days * I am What I Will Be * Shechinah * God the Merciful * Tao * Brachman.

The denominative 'god' points to the mystery and blessedness of life, and allows us to glimpse a dynamic reality which cannot be comprehended by mortal mind. An atheist rightly rejects theism, the idea god is a personal being that blesses some and curses others. Life work of the devout is discerning a universe beyond imagining. This is the impelling force for placing meditation and reflection at the center of our life and work. Vision transcends mortal mind and puts us in an altered state where we may become channels of all that is holy and healing. We access the ganzfeld where meaning is manifest as compassion and justice. The universe is not less than this, nor are we.

When we define divine mind we assume an omnipotent and omniscient force existing in everything and everyone. We envision not a person but a field of energy. In his calling on Mount Horeb, Moses asked god his name. He receives the reply "I am who I am."[35] An alternate translation is "I will be what I will be." In either case this appellation used 43 times in the Old Testament refers to an existential reality not limited by national or ethnic boundaries. Ascription of maleness to god is the inevitable outcome of dualism built into language. Appellation god includes male and female.

God is the superposition of a thousand appellations. Truth is errorless. That which we call god creates, maintains, and sources healing in life. It is blasphemy to assign evil to god. God can do no evil. Put in service to secondary ends, god becomes a tool in the hands of those, who lacking spiritual awareness, show themselves

---

[35]   Exodus 3:14

indifferent to the distress and pain of others. Their desire for power allows them to terrorize others. Jesus was quoting common wisdom when he commented: "by their fruits you shall know them."[36]

In the Newtonian world of cause and effect life appears to be consequent on adequate prior causation lacking pattern and purpose. Astrophysicists report galaxies millions of light years across which appear to function randomly. Within this *mise en scene* earth appears a mere speck of no consequence. At the same time the sidereal world has a haunting elegance. Taken as a whole it manifests breathtaking beauty that challenge human aspirations.

Irony of ironies, Quantum physics turns the world upside down. The deeper you go the more evanescent physical life becomes until finally matter disappears altogether and what is left is energy or life force. There is no vacuum. Space is full of pulsating energy in which sentient life vibrates in harmony. We face the startling reality of atoms jumping in and out of existence and wonder whence they came and where they go. We find ourselves at the center of a startling universe of unimaginable possibilities all of which appear influenced by human consciousness.

Let us test for the presence of the life force. When you quiet retro and neo minds and are without bodily disturbance you align with the ganzfeld and experience peace, equanimity, and joy. You will have a sense of omniscience and participation at the center of the life force. External oriented life driven by desire to wealth, power, and position will recede and be replaced by conscious driven desire to be a source of healing during your limited visit to this life. High-lighting the life force gives meaning to mortality. Rather than manifesting absurdity, our "three score and ten" are basic part of the depth of possibility which sentient life us. This would be no less motive if we lived a thousand years.

Here is a test for the presence of divine mind providing consciousness and guidance. There is a place inside individuals beyond the reach of human mind, which when they access it they can trust themselves to

---

36   Matthew 7:20

bring forth justice, compassion, and healing. It forms the intention for all sentient life on the planet. Inductive insights reveal presence of a higher being. Mortal mind shapes intuitions into moral principles and ethical behavior.

Compassion and personal sacrifice reflects activation in the individual of divine mind. In all religions there are echoes of the Sermon on the Mount expressing centrality of mercy, forgiveness, patience, and purity of heart. Echoing deep inside they empower and compel the enlightened. Divine mind is reflected, albeit imperfectly, in sacred scripture, enshrined in beloved saints, and the lore of a people. Expressed in the arts, song, dance, and poetry gracious acts of kindness bespeaks essential beauty and benignity of divine mind.

There is a grotesquerie in human nature which unmanaged can cause frightful pain and ugliness. Hate, anger and violence within us often appears more compelling than love and forgiveness. Because of the potential for evil within individuals and society the first premise of most theologies asserts the myth of the fall and the assertion of human corruption. It is alleged humankind left to itself is unable to achieve worthwhile value, continuously self-destructs, and because of wickedness is in need of a savior. Every age finds reason to assert human depravity is incontrovertible. Go inside and discover which is more compelling-your desire for light and love, or your inclination to do harm. Find the answer within yourself. Act on it and let consequences convince you.

Inclination of the heart for justice and compassion surfaces in contingent form in physical life. While always possible good is not certain. It must make its way. Sitting aware between mortal mind and divine mind, the aware person continuously chooses light over darkness, good over bad, kin over self, and life over death. By right choices over a lifetime of challenges the believer grows soul. Intentionally he becomes instrument of divine compassion. Acting unrequitedly in behalf of others surely is sign of presence of divine mind and energy. Acting in behalf of others signifies love is both means and ends of cosmic processes.

There is no doubt in human affairs an evolution whereby mortal mind increasingly reflects divine mind. We are deeply moved by those of kindly and generous spirit, the vast dynamic of creation, and our souls delight in beauty. Each of us, to the degree we are aware, has reason to see, sometimes only retrospectively, the hand of god at work in our lives.

> Vision is errorless truth derived from the ganzfeld.
> Cassiopeia on a starry night fills the heart with delight.
> Third movement of Beethoven's Ninth sates soul with joy.
> Committed care by the beloved warms and heals sinews and cells.
> Feral furry friends of the forest are beloved comrades in arms.
> Feathered friends aerate to enchant.
> Then there is pure I am that I am.

Symbolism

Symbolic logic is the study of formal properties of a string of symbols. It examines truth of premises, validity of argument, plus reality of referents. When the referent is conceptually derived you enter the field of virtual reality. Discussion is limited to that which exists as idea. Most conversation takes place in virtual reality. When the referent has a basis in fact, the speaker accesses an existential reality and the nature of discussion changes. It becomes more real and often painful. In this regard the speaker and the subject share something of their being. Speaking in favor of justice and acting justly are two different realities. In the first place there is distance between the concept and the speaker. He is safe "within the box. "His allusions may be far-reaching and exciting at the same time the personal cost is minimal. In the second the speaker comes from a different place inside himself. Recognizing the complexities and costs involved he speaks diffidently and thoughtfully. By his presence he testifies to his willing to pay whatever personal costs may be. Each has his part to play conceptually and effectively. Circumstances will dictate which is called for.

What is meaning? The core concept is that life has meaning. That which we seek is fundamental to existence and not a secondary descriptive overlay. Operating here again is the distinction between existential and virtual reality. That which we seek is both ends and means, physical and metaphysical, concrete and conceptual. We cherish those who at personal cost act to value and maintain life. Life transpires within them and we live by their light. This realization is built into life and the hearts of the righteous.

Moving from mortal mind to divine mind, from duality to singularity makes conversation difficult. Communicating from disparate worlds is hard. To communicate deeper things of reality is a matter of talking less and meditating more. Communication through serenity and repose is truly a pedagogy of silence. Those who with self-control of body and mind establish their own insight and tranquility will discover their own greatness and all that goes with personal integrity. Freed from mortal mind, you will comprehend things which previously were so beyond comprehension they were dismissed as miracles. You will dream unimaginable dreams certain of their reality. You will glimpse parallel universes and shake your head in dumbfounded wonder at that of which you are apart.

Mortal Mind

When the alienated individual feels it necessary to prove himself superior to others, discussion has an Alice in Wonderland aspect: "what I say is true. I do not prevaricate." Mortal mind projects certainty when tentativeness might allow viable differences to be heard and considered. The press of the ego to assert itself is accompanied by drive to diminish others. In a closed system it is just the function of the apparatus. The perceptive person recognizes that faulty reason quickly spirals downward to heightened conflict. Patiently seeking a higher reason he becomes aware of that part of himself not governed by his or others anger. He finds himself able to create a quiet and serene place from which to observe his own and others thinking. Able to see pass the immediate he fashions a conversation where higher possibilities appear for consideration and action.

When his Higher Self is active his desire to harm others has no sway. Seeking first the ground of being he enlists himself in the work to further justice and compassion. For the illumined person it is a process of constant rebirthing. The purpose of life is to strengthen alignment with the intention of the universe to create and maintain life. In his life and conversations he makes clear within himself and others the necessity of an irenic attitude.

Positioned between divine mind and mortal mind the liberated observer chooses for attunement with the principles of life. Following the lower self often it followed by grim consequences. Higher self comes with obstacles of its own. Either path confronts with obstructions and impediments that take the measure of the individual's soul. Whatever the obstacles he is unable to resist the good. Consciousness is not compelled either by inner our outer stimuli. It is the constant mentor of honesty and fairness. In choosing to work for human betterment and peace among nations the individual becomes co-creator of the universe.

Affective State

Feeling is an affective state arising out of emotions, sentiments, or desires that produces a psychic state of pictures, sounds, and bodily sensations. Often taste, touch, and smell are included. Three levels of feeling produces variant results.

Built into the physiology of the individual are instinctive emotions. They include fear, anger, lust and generosity. Sexual craving passing as love adds drama to the human encounter while insuring survival of the species. Primitive emotions are often intense and irrational. Unfortunately, gross feelings in which the untutored operate accounts for much of the non workability in society

The reflective person aware of his involuntary sentiments and desires shapes them to human form. Having examined by touch or searched out the range of emotions the individual molds them to the human situation. Love which previously was raw and ungovernable becomes a reason for committed bonding. When emotions under control we say the individual is judicious or discreet. This is the second level of affective awareness.

Having recognized limitations and pitfalls of cognitive thought an observant individual finds himself viewing life from a shifted perspective. That which before was ordinary shimmers with transcendence. He has direct experience of the affection of the universe for sentient life. In the space of mindlessness the life force manifests joy and meaning. The commonplace is illuminated teeming with possibilities beyond realm of thought. Freed from mortal mind, responsive to divine mind we describe this individual as enlightened. The double entendre is appropriate here.

Depression

In a materialist techno culture with weakening social ties it is not surprising there is a high incidence of psychic depression. When individuation replaces group life, and relationships are marked and measured by fiscal realities it is no wonder families founder. Bereft of intimacy, individuals experience sadness and dejection. Depression is a neurotic state marked by inability to focus attention, reduction of physical vigor, attended with feelings of gloom and hopelessness. Untreated mild neurotic disassociation may descend to psychotic state damaging to individuals intellectual, emotional and physical health. Standing over the coffin of a loved one ponders the central question of life. On hearing of the death of his wife Macbeth absorbed in his thoughts muses:

> Tomorrow, and tomorrow, and tomorrow
> Creeps in this petty pace from day to day,
> To the last syllable of recorded time;
> All our yesterdays have lighted fools
> The way to dusty death. Out, out brief candle!
> Life's but a walking shadow, a poor player
> That struts and frets his hour upon the stage.
> And then is heard no more; it is a tale
> Told by an idiot, full of sound and fury,
> Signifying nothing.[37]

---

[37] Shakespeare Macbeth V v 17

Bereft, Macbeth finds "life's but a walking shadow" lacking both meaning and hope. He proceeds on a course that can only lead to death.

In a state of calm abiding the individual recognizes despondence as part of his retro-mind makeup from which he has the power to free himself. The aware person is able to take full responsibility for his emotional life. Events are the occasion rather than the cause of doom and gloom ideation. It takes practice to liberate the higher self and gain confidence life is not being done to him. Witness consciousness is a major benefit of meditation whereby the person is aware of feelings of despair and hopelessness and at the same time is not controlled by them. Steps to neutralize feelings of dejection and re-establish sense of wholeness and happiness include the following.

Establish Self Awareness.

Opening space between mortal mind and divine mind is fundamental to establishing, integrity, self-respect, and freedom from commercial values of a materialist culture.

Be Non-judgmental And Patient With Self And Others

Experience self as an autonomous being not at the effect of others. With incredible lightness of being the enlightened are able to mildly disassociate from retro-mind to enjoy the irony and humor in life.

Avoid Situations That Increase Hostility And Furtive Behavior.

Don't put yourself at risk. Do what is necessary to maintain distance from destructive attitudes. This is not always possible. Unable to avoid conflict reach deeper into the reservoir of grace see through the immediate to the ganzfeld, and summon healing power to the conflict. While not pleasant, personal trials are often opportunities for great learning.

Reach Out To Those That Care For You.

It is no wonder we deem godlike affection we receive from family and friends. Love is the life force of the universe. Compassion is the same always in all people everywhere. It is the shared conscience of the universe. When you love your neighbor you are healing yourself and vice versa.

Establish A Place Radiating Peace And Comfort.

Create for yourself a place of daily prayer and repose. Over time your space will reflect back your sacred energy. Go there to be healed. Through intention and prayer send healing to distant others. Participate in mending the fabric of the universe. Be prepared to be surprise at what you bring about. There are no coincidences.

Trans-rational Outcomes

It is counter-intuitive to act against self-interest. Yet guided by divine mind and desiring to serve the beloved at whatever cost, individuals often choose to do so. Our hearts are warmed we laud as saints those who sacrifice self for the greater benefit of others.

Keep A Journal Reporting Events And Time Passing

Becoming a citizen of humanity is not for the faint hearted or those with casual commitment to life. It takes self-awareness, discipline and above all willingness to learn from mistakes. Keep a daily journal to capture your discoveries.

Share Learning Appropriately With Others.

Integrity is being grounded in the principles of the universe. It includes active concern for all sentient beings. Sharing insight contributes to the warp and woof of the universe. Everyone, literally everyone, benefits.

The task is to enliven divine mind present in the hearts of men and women. Through meditation and reflection they access the unified field of divine mind in which all things live and move and have their being. Consciousness influences all levels of creation from rocks to cosmic organization. As integral part of the whole each person accepts their duty to live by divine mind and bring about equity and empathy on the planet.

Meditate mind quietly.
Awareness composes consciousness,
Body goes to repose it knows.
Calm body, quiet mind, open heart.
With mind whispers carefully heard,
Divine mind blesses with guidance.
Mortal mind sings in key of bliss,
Unforgeting shining depth of creation,
Always known.
From dubiety to benignity energy shifts,
Into importuning space flows healing.
Intention abandons evanescence,
Enter the domain of ever greatness.

Chapter Nine

Glossary

Concepts are tools we employ to ferret out the substrata of reality. Used wisely, rather than merely descriptive, they lead to an altered state of being. Words conceal as much as they reveal. We amplify vocabulary to deepen our insight. This is particularly true when non-local awareness arrives from distant places.

ACEDIA   Ennui. Spiritual apathy

ANIMA   The unconscious or inner self or soul of the individual as distinguished from the persona or outer aspect of the personality. Sometimes refers to the female aspects of the male personality.

ANTHROPOLOGY Teaching concerning the genesis, nature, and destiny of human beings.

ANTHROPOSOPHY A spiritual investigation pursued with the same rigor as the physical sciences. Through inner development an individual can obtain objective and comprehensive knowledge of the spirit world.

A POSTERIORI   Arguing from facts or particulars to general principles. From effects to causes. Inductive. Empirical.

APOCALYPSE   The Book of Revelation portends planetary doom. It contains symbolic visions of the immanent total and complete destruction of the world.

A PRIORI   Based on an assumed theory or hypothesis with no supporting experimental evidence. Proceeding from a known cause to a presumed necessary effect. Deductive from a first premise.

ARMAGEDDON   The final and decisive battle on earth between good and evil in which the righteous prevail.

BEG THE QUESTION   To evade or dodge the real issue.

CHAKRA   In Buddhism one of seven energy ports within the body.

CLEMENCY   Disposition to show mercy toward an enemy.

CHRISTADELPHIAN   Brother of Christ.

COGNITION   The mental process of knowing. It includes levels of awareness, perception, reason, and judgment.

CONSCIOUSNESS   An altered state of objective awareness of ones attitudes, beliefs, thoughts, and feelings. Action in managing mental processes and creating alternatives to mortal mind.

CONTINGENCY   An event that may occur but is not likely or intended. Uncertainty. Condition of being dependent on chance. Something incidental to something else.

DE REGUEUR   Socially obligatory

DISASSOCIATION   Detach from external reality. Functions in a habitual way. Unable to unlearn inherited or learned patterns and take on new behavior. Develops mental strategies of deception, prevarication, equivocation, and subterfuge to keep the game in play.

DOUBLE TALK   Deliberatively evasive or beside the point as to be meaningless. Also referred to as "begging the question."

DYSTOPIA   A place or state in which conditions are extremely grim or dire.

EGO MIND   Refers to specific content and composition of individual mind. It may be our best friend or worst enemy.

ENCHIRIDION a textbook or manual.

ENLIGHTENMENT   To be guided by spiritual insight. A state of being in which the individual receives unmediated knowledge, transcends suffering and desire, experience unity with the life force. Bliss.

ENTROPY   Tendency of all matter and energy in the universe to evolve to a state of inert uniformity. An inevitable and steady deterioration of a system or society. A measure of the disorder or randomness of a closed system

EVERSION   Turing inside out.

EXISTENTIAL   Relating to or dealing fact or state of being. Existence when experienced has both a universal and empirical quality.

FAITH   Acceptance what is known in the heart to be true. Larger than intellectual assent, faith is awareness of and commitment to the higher self. Faith is a creative act that informs reason. It is human response to the increasing consciousness of the World.

FIELD   A field is a region of influence. A matrix or medium that connects two or more points in space by a force such as gravity or electromagnetism having a determinable value in every point of the region.

FORTUITOUS   Happening by accident or change, either good or bad.

FUNGIBLE Interchangeable

GANZFELD German for 'whole field' is one vast sea of energy filling up the space between things. An invisible web connecting everything to everything else.

GENIUS LOCI   The distinctive pervading spirit of the place. The guardian deity.

GENOCIDE   Planned and systematic extermination of an entire national, ethnic, racial, or political group.

GNOSTICISM   Gnosis is apprehension of extraordinary, unmediated, non-local knowledge. Intuition is available to the pure of heart whose aim is to enlarge the spiritual element in mankind. It is often associated with dualism wherein matter is considered imperfect and antagonistic to the metaphysical nature of man.

GRACE   Divine love and protection freely bestowed on mankind. State of being sanctified and protected by the Almighty. Gracious is disposition characterized by mercy, generosity, and clemency.

INTENTION OF THE UNIVERSE   Design and evolutionary movement are fundamental to the universe. Built-in purpose and goals include manifestation of beauty and disposition toward compassion.

KARMA   In Buddhism the law of cause and effect as pertains to the spiritual world. The total effect of a persons speech and action which determines his destiny over multiple life-times.

LIFE FORCE is the fundamental energetic reality that composes 94% of the universe and is open to influence by conscious individuals. Life force reveals itself as love.

LOCUTION   A particular word, phrase, or expression used by a particular person or group. A style of speaking or phraseology.

LOGOS   Logos means "word" and is one of the many names of God. In John 1:1 Logos is the creative word of God incarnate in Jesus. Governing principle of the universe.

MAYA   Transitory, variegated appearance of the sensible world which obscures the undifferentiated spiritual wholeness from which it arose. The illusory appearance of the physical world.

MEANING   Concept, knowledge, or term reflecting what lies behind the physical apart from concrete existence. The inner significance of things.

MEDITATION   Process of inward attention and discovery that frees the individual from transitory positional thinking.

MATERIALISM   Theory that physical matter, governed by mechanistic laws of cause-and-effect is the only reality. Everything in the universe can be explained in terms of physical phenomenon.

META-COGNITIVE   Beyond and transcending the ordinary processes of perception, reason, and judgment.

METAPHYSICS A priori speculation about matters that remains unanswerable to scientific observation, analysis, and experiment. The examination of the nature of reality including relationship between mind and matter, fact and value, substance and attribute.

METEMPSYCHOSIS   Reincarnation.

NEO MIND Thought process with here and now orientation. Focus on contemporary events their causes and consequences.

NEURO-LINGUISTICS   Study of visual, auditory, kinesthetic, olfactory, and gustatory representational systems that compose thought processes.

NONLOCALITY The ability of an electron to instantaneously influence another particle over distance without exchange of force or energy. Matter is a complex web of interdependent relationships forever indivisible.

OBSERVER   That part of the individual liberated from mortal mind and accessing the spiritual undergirding of reality. Creates an altered state accompanied with a shifted perspective of perception, judgment, and action.

PEDAGOGY   The art or method of teaching.

PLACEHOLDER   In a complex equation or logical expression a word, symbol, or name may replace any element or the total set.

PRECONSCIOUS MIND   Ideas, feelings, attitudes not within immediate awareness. Source of thought. Also called retro-mind, mortal mind, pre-mind, hind mind, and unconscious mind.

PROBABILITY   Likelihood something will happen based on indeterminable factors like randomness or chance.

POSSIBILITY   Capable of happening but of uncertain likelihood.

QUANTUM PHYSICS   Contemporary physical science theory of wave/particle duality. 94% of the universe is energy. Remaining part is matter. The universe is far more mysterious that mankind has imagined.

RATIONALIZATION   Creation of a false or incorrect reason for doing what you want to do for other reasons. Self-satisfying but dubious explanation for ones behavior.

RAISON DE'ETRE   Reason or justification for being

REIKE Metaphysical technique for stress reduction and relaxation that promotes healing.

REMISSIBLE   Being such forgiveness is possible.

RETRO-MIND A generic term for thinking sourced in the past. Unconscious mind is backward looking .Retrospective and often reactive.

SACERDOTAL   Relating to priests or priesthood.

SATORI   State of spiritual enlightenment.

SCHADENFREUDE   Malicious glee derived from pain of others.

SEALED   Mormon doctrine marriage is eternal.

SINE QUA NON   An essential element or condition. That without which there is nothing.

SOLIPSISM   The idea the self is the only thing that can be known and verified. Leads to circular thinking. "If I say a thing three times it's true."

SOLITUDINARIAN   One who lives a secluded life.

SOUL   The animating and vital principle of human beings. An immaterial entity that was never born and cannot die. Through soul higher beings communicate with mortals.

SUI GENERIS   Being the only example of its kind.

SUPERPOSITION   Designation of a symbol included in a set and placing it at the head as referring to and including all its parts.

TAO   The pathless path of spiritual growth.

THEANTHROPISM   Attribution of human traits to God. Doctrine of the union of human and divine natures in Jesus and all mankind.

VIRTUAL REALITY A simulated reality that exists in concept only. Often computer driven to create an artificial environment for study. In complex situations rationalizations are created to explain what lives only in argument and is not objectively verifiable.

WITNESS CONSCIOUSNESS   An altered state in which the individual no longer passive to thinking chooses to acknowledge and pursue his higher calling.

ZEITGEIST   The spirit of the time. Ideation and outlook of a generation.

ZERO POINT FIELD Ambient ground state energy field. Basic substratum of the universe and repository all ground energy, and all virtual particles. All matter is connected to the furthest reaches of the universe.

Words place us in different perspectives.   Maya, myth, and monism represent different thought worlds.   Remember you create your universe. Use them in your efforts to bring forth what you desire for yourself and others.

R. Dudley Bennett
16 Warwick Way
Jackson, New Jersey 08527
((732) 833-7631

Mr. Bennett graduated from Ottawa Hills High School Grand Rapids Michigan received his BA degree from Calvin College in 1950. He enlisted in the military. Discovering a college graduate in the ranks the Army sent him to Cadre School at Fort Leonard Wood, Missouri and Officer Candidate School. He graduated from The Army General School, Fort Riley Kansas in 1953. As Assistant Operations Officer Regimental Headquarters, Lt. Bennett spent two years at Aberdeen Proving Ground Maryland.

In 1956 Mr. Bennett graduated from Berkeley Center Yale Divinity School. Parochial responsibilities included Greenville, Michigan where he created Sunshine Camp for rural poor children and New Paltz, New York where he organized the Ulster Country Community Chest. Rev. Bennett became Chaplain of Rutgers University Newark. Between 1963-68 he completed 33 hours of graduate work in Sociology at the New Brunswick Campus

Mr. Bennett was a Founding Director and Corporate Secretary of City National Bank of New Jersey for 15 years. He brought Self Help and Resource Exchange (SHARE) to New Jersey in 1985. During 40 years of proprietorship with wife Margaret and children Paul, Martha, and Sarah, of The Orchard School, West Caldwell, New Jersey over 1800 pre-school children began their education.

During 20 years as President of American National Training he consulted with and trained management in over 50 American Corporations. He specialized in Team Building, Management Development, and Organizational Interfacing. Clients included IBM, Ford Motor, Bank of New York, Westvaco, FMC, US Army. His TA and The Manager (ISBN 0-8144-5422-4) was published by American Management Association in 1978 and translated into German and Danish. Successful Team Building appeared in 1980. (ISBN 0-8144-5607-3) Pedagogy In Silence in 2008 (ISBN978-1-4343-4972-9). Rebirthing The American Dream, dedicated to President Barack Obama will be published late in 2009,

www.ingramcontent.com/pod-product-compliance
Lightning Source LLC
Chambersburg PA
CBHW031240280526
45784CB00004B/1660